WHITE HOUSE
CROSSWORDS

★ ★ ★ DAVID J. KAHN ★ ★ ★

PUZZLE
WRIGHT
PRESS

New York

PUZZLE WRIGHT PRESS

New York

An Imprint of Sterling Publishing
1166 Avenue of the Americas
New York, NY 10036

ISBN 978-1-4549-1505-8

Distributed in Canada by Sterling Publishing
℅ Canadian Manda Group, 664 Annette Street
Toronto, Ontario, Canada M6S 2C8
Distributed in the United Kingdom by GMC Distribution Services
Castle Place, 166 High Street, Lewes, East Sussex, England BN7 1XU
Distributed in Australia by Capricorn Link (Australia) Pty. Ltd.
P.O. Box 704, Windsor, NSW 2756, Australia

For information about custom editions, special sales, and premium
and corporate purchases, please contact Sterling Special Sales
at 800-805-5489 or specialsales@sterlingpublishing.com.

Manufactured in Canada

2 4 6 8 10 9 7 5 3 1

www.puzzlewright.com

CONTENTS

INTRODUCTION

United States presidents have always intrigued me, and not only because of their successes and failures. Who knew that Calvin Coolidge was the only president sworn in by his father, that Jimmy Carter was the first president born in a hospital, and that some of George Washington's speeches were written by Alexander Hamilton? Yes, many presidents did and said odd or funny things, had interesting hobbies, and were given colorful nicknames. There is a wealth of material buried in the history books that lends itself to crosswords.

You don't have to be a history buff to enjoy this collection of 40 creative, funny, and entertaining crosswords. They start off easy and get slightly harder as you go along, but none are especially hard to solve. I think you'll have as much fun solving these puzzles as I had writing them.

—David J. Kahn

COMING TO TERMS

ACROSS
1 Blackboard marker
6 Performed an aria
10 Newspaper piece
14 Is wearing
15 "Peek-___!"
16 Sniffer
17 "Get ___!"
18 Remove from a mother's milk
19 *Born Free* lioness
20 Item on a marriage certificate?
23 Ryan of *When Harry Met Sally*
24 Him: French
25 Throw ___ (rant)
26 Insurance coverage for a housekeeper?
32 Paintings and the like
33 Misery
34 Pool player's stick
35 Conduits
38 Big shot, for short
39 Sail supports
41 Volcanic debris
42 Dads
43 "My gal" of song
44 Unwanted surprise after a tribal leader's rain dance?
50 Bank offering
51 Ewe's sound
52 Bill, after a president's signature
54 Dodgers general manager Rickey who signed Jackie Robinson?
59 Drip from a pipe, e.g.
60 Privy to
61 Supreme Court justice Samuel
62 *The Diary of ___ Frank*
63 Etching liquid
64 Canadian music awards
65 Bringing up the rear
66 Rogues
67 Love, Italian-style

DOWN
1 Deep gap
2 Stopped
3 Hard Italian cheese
4 Place to store hay
5 Soon-to-be knights, e.g.
6 Deemed appropriate
7 Help in crime
8 Biblical ark builder
9 Blown a gasket
10 Score of the 2014 World Cup final
11 Topic often discussed by TV pundits
12 Petrol brand
13 JFK cabinet member Rusk
21 Give the heave-ho
22 Sci-fi vehicle
27 Wrestling surface

28 "Wouldn't that be nice!"
29 Police officer
30 Abridge
31 "I agree"
35 "Lah-di-___!"
36 Red, white, and blue initials
37 Valparaiso natives
38 Winery container
39 Hindu prince

40 Boxer known as "The Greatest"
42 Old Firebird car maker
43 Strikebreaker
45 Charm on a necklace
46 Greek letter after sigma
47 Corrects
48 Pacific weather phenomenon

49 Ingredient
53 "___ side are you on anyway?"
54 Airline to Israel
55 TV's warrior princess
56 Ancient Peruvian
57 Null and ___
58 JFK, in relation to Harvard

WHO KNEW?

ACROSS

1 Capital of Peru
5 Gave up, as territory
10 Bygone Iran leader
14 "'Tis a pity"
15 Pop concert venue
16 Bullfighter's red cloak
17 *Sesame Street* friend of Ernie
18 James Madison once accused Benjamin Franklin of being a ___
20 Decorative pond fish
22 Heart
23 Brewery product
24 Agent's take: Abbr.
26 Franklin D. Roosevelt's last inaugural address lasted about ___
30 Ocean at maximum ebb
32 Noggin
33 "This guy walks into ___ ..." (joke opener)

34 Walk-___ (small movie roles)
36 Treeless plain
40 Musical chord
42 Underworld boss
44 Word after long or dog
45 Bicycle for two
47 Feathery scarf
49 Desertlike
50 The Clintons, in law school
52 Prods
54 Calvin Coolidge wrote a will consisting of ___
58 "___ been real!"
59 ___ Harbour, Florida
60 Stadium level
61 Was out in front
63 John Tyler fathered a child at ___
67 Take a siesta
70 Big truck maker
71 Similar
72 Poker pot starter
73 Many a U.S. president: Abbr.

74 Kremlin denials
75 River of Hades

DOWN

1 Research room
2 ___ du Diable
3 Franklin D. Roosevelt took the term "new deal" from a novel by ___
4 Regarding
5 Taxi
6 Blow it
7 Clear, as a windshield in winter
8 Bury
9 Some Wisconsin farms
10 Educ. institution
11 Attacks
12 iMac maker
13 President Garfield's predecessor
19 Where Andrew Johnson served before and after his presidency
21 "___ Had a Hammer"
24 Oliver of *The West Wing*

25 Mongoose's enemy
27 Wedding words
28 Sell
29 Nervousness
31 Buys and sells
35 Cry loudly
37 Thomas Jefferson's self-written epitaph didn't mention that he had been ___
38 Ross who founded the Reform Party

39 Idyllic places
41 End key neighbor
43 Word that's an example of itself
46 Honda Odyssey, e.g.
48 Javelin's path
51 Like a cold, hard gaze
53 Hair spiffer-upper
54 #44 in the presidential history books

55 Bother persistently
56 President-___
57 Cubs legend Banks
62 Time periods
64 Heavens
65 Depot purchase: Abbr.
66 "Sure thing"
68 Home in the mud
69 Where President Eisenhower was born: Abbr.

ACTING PRESIDENTIAL

ACROSS
1 In ___ land (spacy)
5 Biblical wise men
9 List of candidates
14 "Maybe ___ help"
15 Like some vaccines
16 Lugged
17 Hoodlum
18 Franklin D. Roosevelt, in 2012's *Hyde Park on Hudson*
20 Sharpened
22 "I cannot tell ___" (Washington quote)
23 Big rabbit features
24 Lots and lots
26 With 12-Down, running wild
27 Theodore Roosevelt, in 2006's *Night at the Museum*
34 Fannie ___ (1930s federal program to aid banks)

36 Exxon product
37 Dental filling
38 With 41-Across, John Quincy Adams, in 1997's *Amistad*
41 See 38-Across
43 Hooked to a wrecker, e.g.
44 Butter holder
45 In good physical shape
46 Lyndon B. Johnson, in 2013's *The Butler*
51 Sheep's cry
52 Deli meat
55 "Regrettably ..."
59 Land of leprechauns
61 Rubbernecker, e.g.
62 George W. Bush, in 2008's *W.*
65 Falafel bread
66 Fond farewell
67 Carson's successor
68 Politician's goal
69 "Old Rough and ___" (Zachary Taylor's nickname)

70 Sketched
71 Writer ___ Stanley Gardner

DOWN
1 Certain art print, for short
2 Sneeze sound
3 *My Beautiful ___* (Daniel Day-Lewis movie)
4 San ___, Texas
5 Unruly crowd
6 Opera diva's song
7 Site for a hanging, in westerns
8 The Big Ten's Fighting ___
9 Symington who was a 1960 presidential contender
10 Oral history
11 Gillette razor brand
12 See 26-Across
13 Ice cream brand
19 Brunch or dinner

21 Belle of the ball, for short

25 Aries or Leo

28 Aye's opposite

29 Gloss-y place?

30 Tattoo fluid

31 Classic boxing rivalry, familiarly

32 ___-pedi (spa treatment)

33 The "S" in GPS: Abbr.

34 Postal delivery

35 Years, in Latin

39 ___ lane (commuters' aid)

40 Pained cries

41 Color

42 Japanese sashes

44 Movie preview

47 Trucker with a handle

48 Playwright Pinter

49 Piece of luggage

50 Go by, as time

53 Iron or tin

54 Really mad

55 Slightly open

56 Rich supply of ore

57 It's east of Europe

58 Tool building

60 Supreme Court number

63 Wall Street order

64 This minute

FIRST OF ALL

ACROSS
1 Prove suitable for
6 Madison Avenue exec
11 Monk's title
14 Make amends
15 Dolphins' city
16 Lowe of *The West Wing*
17 George Washington's longtime home
19 ___ and flow
20 President Obama's mother
21 One who closely resembles another
22 Leg joint
23 Resolutely
25 Disparage openly
26 Amino and citric
28 Strength
29 Chinese secret society
30 Some knives
34 1950s presidential candidate's monogram
36 Wild revelry
37 Father-and-son presidential name
38 *To Live and Die* ___
39 Like Beethoven's *Pastoral* Symphony
40 Musical staff members
41 Lyric poems
42 Its capital is Cardiff
44 Pigs' digs
45 Lab glove material
46 Certain infielder
50 K-12, in education lingo
51 He came to power during Eisenhower's second term
52 Society girl, briefly
55 Taproom order
56 Site of Washington's first inauguration (in 1789)
58 Knight's title
59 Time waster
60 Fill with joy
61 Suffix with baron
62 Irritable
63 Has supper

DOWN
1 Crimson Tide, to fans
2 English school founded in 1440
3 Washington was one of them
4 Quaint lodging
5 Aquarium favorites
6 Prayer endings
7 Sad song
8 *Olympia* painter Edouard
9 Roman god of love
10 Writer Anaïs
11 With 32-Down, start of Washington's military career
12 Distant relative of Martha Washington

13 Monk's residence

18 Kid-___ (children's shows)

22 Beer holder

24 Irritable

25 Talk smack about

26 Yours: French

27 British general defeated by Washington at Yorktown

28 Can of worms

30 *A Christmas Carol* cries

31 Harem room

32 See 11-Down

33 Little devil

35 Smart talk

38 Itsy-bitsy bit

40 Gender

43 Hawaiian garland

44 Puffed on a cigarette

45 Rent

46 Cries one's eyes out

47 Until now

48 Tale

49 Mess up

51 Surrender

53 Suffix with major

54 Tournament passes

56 Trivial complaint

57 151, in old Rome

FUNNY FINISHES

ACROSS

1 In the middle of
6 The Bruins of the NCAA
10 One-spot card
13 Back tooth
14 Symbol of slowness
15 Fall behind
16 "I have left orders to be awakened at any time in case of national emergency— even if I'm in ___": Reagan
19 Spine-tingling
20 *Lucky Jim* author Kingsley
21 "Better to remain silent and be thought a fool than to speak out and ___": Lincoln
27 Made level
28 Quantity: Abbr.
29 City in Colombia
30 Finnish bath
33 Battery type
36 "I only know two tunes: one of them is 'Yankee Doodle' ___": Grant
40 Letter writer's afterthoughts
41 Someone ___ (not mine)
42 Director Preminger
43 Cry from a crib
44 Encourage
46 "If I were two-faced, would I be ___?": Lincoln
51 Male turkeys
52 Burr who was Jefferson's vice president
53 "I hear that I'm still pretty big on Twitter, Facebook—or as Sarah Palin calls it, the ___": Obama
60 Juice suffix
61 Flood preventer
62 Aquafina rival
63 Seedy bread
64 Nourish
65 Mary Poppins, for one

DOWN

1 Doctors' org.
2 Slip-on shoe, for short
3 Suffix with plug
4 Arrest
5 Be sorrowful
6 "___ we meet again"
7 Desert animal
8 Untruth
9 Malt beverage
10 Out on ___ (vulnerable)
11 "That's enough talk!"
12 Hen products
14 Song word repeated after "Que"
17 Scholarship basis
18 Tense
21 Postgame wrap-up
22 1916 presidential candidate Charles ___ Hughes
23 Blends
24 "I'm working ___"

25 Hamlet, by nationality
26 Sharif of *Doctor Zhivago*
30 Emergency call
31 Had breakfast
32 Sounds of doubt
33 Houston baseballer
34 Composer Bruckner
35 Do penance
37 Listen to
38 For grades 1 to 12
39 Some markers
43 "What ___ thinking?"
44 Like show horses' feet
45 Bowlers, old-style
46 *Annie Hall* director Allen
47 Toastmaster
48 Unsophisticated
49 Stared intently
50 Word with shoe or family
51 Old Russian ruler
54 1936 presidential candidate Landon
55 Grant's Civil War opponent
56 Actress Longoria
57 Ruckus
58 007 creator Fleming
59 One or more

FOUR-TIMER

ACROSS

1 Curved path
4 Lessened, as pain
9 Steven Bochco TV drama
14 "Fat chance!"
15 Campfire treat
16 City northwest of Orlando
17 School's URL ending
18 Site of a 1941 attack that prompted a famous 36-Down speech
20 ___ Force One
21 ER workers
22 Stop listening
23 Not sailing
25 Identify
26 Highways: Abbr.
27 Big bother
29 Put two and two together
31 Jockey's straps
33 McGregor of The Impossible
35 Many an Iraqi
39 Kutcher's role on That '70s Show
40 36-Down, familiarly
41 Snoozer's sound
42 Earthen pot
43 Flower's support
44 Govt. bill
45 Used a stool
47 First pro team to play on artificial turf
49 Actress Thurman
52 Laze
54 Trojan War hero
57 Wood of Hollywood
59 Light switch positions
60 George H.W. Bush, e.g.
61 Part of 36-Down's economic recovery program
63 Presidential time interval
64 Rub out
65 Political topic
66 On fire
67 Los ___, California
68 Comes to an end
69 Golf bag item

DOWN

1 Leading in the polls
2 Medium for 36-Down's "fireside chats"
3 British ally of 36-Down during World War II
4 After-dinner drink
5 Changes, as the Constitution
6 In order (to)
7 Goof
8 River mouth feature
9 Gave for a while
10 Farming unit
11 Voting bloc that supported 36-Down
12 For all to hear
13 Witches' blemishes
19 Only ___ (imperfect)
24 Where President Eisenhower grew up

25 36-Down's economic recovery program

28 Political wing, with "the"

30 Rival brand of Yoplait

31 Early MGM rival

32 Snakelike fish

34 Warfare supply

36 #32 in the presidential history books

37 *Thomas Jefferson: The ___ of Power* (Jon Meacham biography)

38 Insect that performs a waggle dance

41 Emphasizes

43 Not reacting

46 United States's side during World War II

48 Get ready for a long car ride

49 Remove wooden pins from

50 Tierney of *ER*

51 Facing the pitcher

53 Jerry or Jerry Lee

55 Eagle's nest

56 ___ of the Union address

58 Too

59 Approximately

62 German direction

FIVE OF A KIND

ACROSS
1 Not digital
7 In the style of, on menus
10 ___ A to Z
14 Weather event whose name means "the girl" in Spanish
15 *20th president*
17 Thinks out loud
18 Giants of Greek myth
19 After-bath powder
20 Ponies up
22 Occupied
23 Actor Wilson
25 Spirited horse
26 How some rooms are lit
29 *18th president*
32 Conducted
35 Dress with a flared bottom
36 Run-down
37 Suffix with labyrinth
38 Dispose (of)
39 The end
40 "Silent ___" (Coolidge's nickname)

41 Creation of Congress
42 Charms
43 Beaded counters
45 Sidewalk stand drink
46 *19th president*
47 Lets or sublets
48 Good name for a Dalmatian
50 Eisenhower's alma mater: Abbr.
52 Bone: Prefix
54 Senate tie-breaker, slangily
56 Italia's capital
60 Least expensive
62 President Jackson or Johnson
64 *23rd president*
65 Attaches, as a rope
66 Has
67 Place for a mudbath
68 Supports, as a college fund

DOWN
1 Tons
2 California wine valley
3 Indigo dye
4 *16th president*
5 Washington bill
6 Quebec's ___ Peninsula
7 The "A" in CIA: Abbr.
8 Brand of potato chips
9 Hyperbola part
10 "Criminal" singer Apple
11 Like the five presidents with italicized clues
12 Cheers for toreros
13 Store goods: Abbr.
16 Coquettish
21 In an indignant way
24 ___ accord (Bill Clinton achievement)
25 Aardvark's prey
26 Love interest of Alfalfa

27 Epic written by Homer
28 Like the five presidents with italicized clues
30 Title in India
31 Up for discussion
33 Pass, as legislation
34 Places for heros
39 Decree

42 Funny Goldberg
43 Provide with guns
44 Like the five presidents with italicized clues
49 Compote fruit
51 Sudden outpouring
52 ___ Rios, Jamaica

53 1925 Literature Nobelist
54 Abbr. on a bottle of Courvoisier
55 Sicilian volcano
57 Guesstimate phrase
58 Copy cats?
59 Plant bristles
61 Hook shape
63 Famous diarist

STANFORD ENGINEER

ACROSS

1 FDR or LBJ: Abbr.
4 Doc bloc
7 Russian counterpart of the CIA
10 Hole in one
13 Cold cube
14 *Amadeus* antagonist Antonio ___
16 Too permissive
17 ___ long way
18 Length of a short movie, maybe
19 VW predecessors?
20 Picnic pest
21 Kind of gland
22 With 32-Across, Giants slugger
23 Capital of Kansas
25 Casual top
27 "Mamma ___!"
28 Give more cushioning
32 See 22-Across
33 Even so
34 Compassionate words
35 "Sez ___?"
36 Result of poor service, sometimes
37 Sue Grafton's ___ *for Quarry*
40 Cloudless
41 Statute
44 Popular card game
45 German writer Hermann ___
46 "Nope"
47 1960s dance
49 Isn't greedy
52 1950s White House nickname
53 All together
57 Salsa or guacamole
58 Podded plant
59 Broadcast problem during transmission
60 Laudatory poem
61 Blunder
62 Requests
63 Buddhist sect
64 Old military draft org.
65 Born: French
66 JFK's first naval appointment: Abbr.
67 Grain in Cheerios

DOWN

1 Probe persistently
2 It collapsed during the 8-Down
3 Baked dish in *Sweeney Todd*
4 Drenched
5 Language sometimes spoken by Herbert Hoover and his wife
6 Tiger or Ranger, informally
7 Razor-sharp
8 Event that started during Hoover's presidency
9 Laws-to-be

10 He lost to Hoover in the 1928 presidential election
11 Indulge
12 Jump for joy
15 Wrath
24 Down a sub?
26 Anagram of 35-Across
29 French school
30 Cracker spreads
31 Diva offerings
37 Hoover's religious group
38 Crying
39 Not worth a ___
41 Santa ___ winds
42 Supreme Court justice appointed by Hoover
43 "Some nerve!"
47 Nursery supplies
48 Family car
50 Misters, in Mannheim
51 Paid out
54 Manufacture
55 Election campaign spots
56 Not threatened

Answer, page 90

ONE FOR THE BOOKS

ACROSS

1 Massachusetts site of John F. Kennedy's presidential library
7 In the past
10 Horse's gait
14 ___ mama (rum drink)
15 They're in the army now
17 "Enough!"
18 New York site of Franklin D. Roosevelt's presidential library
19 "___ well" (George Washington's last words)
21 "Pronto!"
22 Pretend to be, at a costume party
26 White House chief of staff, e.g.
28 Hooch holder
32 Arkansas site of Bill Clinton's presidential library
36 ___ *Holden* (1900 novel)
37 Soothe
38 "Scat!"
40 Driving hazard
41 Virginia site of Thomas Jefferson's presidential library
45 Charged particle
46 Cleveland's lake
47 Delighted in
48 Claudia ___ Taylor (Lady Bird Johnson's name at birth)
50 California site of Richard M. Nixon's presidential library
53 Dissolve out by percolation
55 Footlong, e.g.
56 Start of a plant
57 Prompted
60 Exxon product
62 Virginia site of Woodrow Wilson's presidential library
66 This evening, in ads
71 Like the New York City metropolitan area
72 Submits a tax return via computer
73 Combustible pile
74 Destiny
75 Texas site of George W. Bush's presidential library

DOWN

1 Air gun ammo
2 Granola bit
3 *Homeland* network, for short
4 Faucet
5 Leave out
6 Indigenous
7 Burnt part
8 *The Naked Maja* painter
9 Automaker Ransom Eli ___
10 Be a boozer
11 Actor Stephen of *The Crying Game*
12 Hockey legend Bobby
13 "Shame on you!"
16 Unable to hear
20 ___ Lancelot

22 Cold as 40-Across

23 Lubrication point

24 Georgia site of Jimmy Carter's presidential library

25 Phone button

27 Campaign items

29 Kansas site of Dwight D. Eisenhower's presidential library

30 Shut off

31 Patella protector

33 Singer Lovett

34 Revolutionary icon's name

35 Bout-ending hits, for short

39 ___ Office

42 Suffix with contradict

43 Uncle: Spanish

44 "Really?"

49 Charge with a crime

51 Locust, say

52 Lessened

54 Scavenge (for)

58 And others: Abbr.

59 Inflict upon

61 Couch

62 Racecar fuel additive

63 Attempt

64 What the EPA monitors

65 Badminton barrier

67 Nothing

68 Sick

69 Tetley product

70 Beginning of summer?

CINCINNATI'S RIDER

ACROSS
1 Got up
6 Edinburgh native
10 Tied
14 Speakers' places
15 Record for later viewing, in a way
16 Ready to be eaten
17 Ecstasy's opposite
18 Winnebago owner, informally
19 Big name in PCs
20 Publisher of Ulysses S. Grant's memoirs
22 Sought answers from
23 Leaky tire sound
24 Fence part
25 Bedazzles
26 Estate attorney's document

28 Cave dweller
31 Swung around
34 Hoopla
35 Osso ___ (veal dish)
36 Grant military foe, 1861–65
40 Somewhat
41 Tractor-trailer
42 Wise old heads
43 "Tippecanoe and Tyler ___" (1840 campaign catchphrase)
44 Study of heredity
47 Addiction
49 *Peter Pan* pooch
50 Certain sib
53 Bygone airline
55 Grant's alma mater
57 Blown saves often make them go up
58 Apple center
59 Mosaic, e.g.
60 It means nothing in tennis
61 Rime

62 Oliver who directed *JFK*, *Nixon*, and *W.*
63 Breyers competitor
64 Woes
65 Red Sea parter

DOWN
1 Sends unwanted emails
2 Forum attire
3 Scents
4 Pigpen sound
5 Gamble on the stock market, maybe
6 ___ of Gibraltar
7 Grant, notably
8 Pizzeria fixture
9 Rocky hill
10 Wipe away
11 1863 Grant military victory site
12 Fencing weapon
13 Uncool sort
21 "What ___ I saying?"
22 Piercing tool
25 Very much

26 Not right?
27 President McKinley's wife
29 Pinnacle
30 Santa's sackful
31 "Go away!"
32 Gray wolf
33 Blockader of Southern ports, 1861–65
35 Sheep bleats

37 1857's ___ Scott Decision
38 German article
39 Avoidance of reality
44 Little beauty
45 Stun guns
46 QB's mistake: Abbr.
48 Lets up
50 Missile sites
51 Silly

52 Eye sores
53 One-named soccer legend
54 Three-time A.L. MVP, in headlines
55 Cashmere, e.g.
56 Aware of
58 Hillary Clinton's hometown, for short

Answer, page 94

JUST THE FACTS

ACROSS

1 Mouth off to
5 Dig find
10 Apple offering
14 Not written
15 You might RSVP online to one
16 First James Bond movie
17 "Beetle Bailey" dog
18 Prosthetics worn by George Washington, mistakenly thought to be made of wood
20 What Theodore Roosevelt's 1905 inaugural address didn't mention even once
22 Cereal bit
23 Tint
24 "I'm outta here"
25 Spot for a hoop
29 Bert's buddy
31 Medium for a weekly presidential address
33 ___ v. Wade
34 Baton Rouge sch.
36 Commanded
37 Sow's squeal
38 When Theodore Roosevelt's mother and first wife both died, in 1884
42 Doesn't feel well
43 Pen name
44 Diplomatic front?
45 Longtime White House correspondent Donaldson
46 Wind indicators
48 Theodore Roosevelt's second wife
52 Issue that led to the American Civil War
54 1960s–1970s White House name
56 Grand ___ (wine designation)
57 Singer ___ King Cole
58 Emperor whose 1804 coronation was attended by James Monroe
60 The first one was ordered built by President Taft
64 Be next to
65 "Good going!"
66 Cruise ship
67 Wear a long face
68 Direction the Lincoln Memorial faces
69 Follows orders
70 Gave the boot

DOWN

1 Provide comfort to
2 President who succeeded Garfield
3 Shiny fabric
4 School zone sign
5 Cook, as beans
6 Escapee
7 1953 Leslie Caron title role
8 "___ the economy, stupid" (1992 campaign catchphrase)
9 So-so grade
10 Perfect
11 South African city
12 Tiny sugar-lover

13 Cry from Homer Simpson
19 Bullring bull
21 Big, big, big
25 Biblical spot
26 Gave support
27 Overly thin
28 "Horrors!"
30 Troubles
32 Theodore Roosevelt's daughter or first wife
35 Open, as a gate
37 Took too much, briefly
38 Lab container
39 Fact-filled books
40 Wee
41 Look after
42 Idiot
46 Presidential power
47 *House of Cards* star Kevin
49 Fridge, old-style
50 Traveling actors' group
51 Went on a safari
53 White House wardrobe aide
55 They do impressions
58 William Henry Harrison, in the presidential history books
59 Tibetan monk
60 *Marine* ___ (presidential helicopter)
61 By way of
62 Good name for a plumber
63 Bit of baloney

ON THE CAMPAIGN TRAIL

ACROSS

1 Busybody
6 Fresh kid
10 Is no longer
13 "Who ___ thunk it?"
14 Seeks political office
15 With 16-Across, lover of souped-up cars
16 See 15-Across
17 1952 Eisenhower campaign slogan
19 79, for gold: Abbr.
20 Swarm (with)
21 Bickering
22 Where things may disappear into
25 Stadium sounds
27 With 45-Across, 1916 Wilson campaign slogan
29 Kitty ___
33 "For ___ sake!"
35 Menacing look
36 1948 Truman campaign slogan

41 Word with horse or space
42 Stainless ___
43 How typical pregnancies are carried
45 See 27-Across
50 Minute part of a minute: Abbr.
52 Tugboat rope
53 The Magi, e.g.
56 Autocrat deposed during Carter's presidency
58 Knowing, as a secret
59 2008 Obama campaign slogan
61 ___ Mae, program since Lyndon B. Johnson's presidency
63 Crony
64 In the cellar
65 V-8, e.g.
66 Flamenco shout
67 Run for it
68 Beginning

DOWN

1 Relieve
2 Pest, in Yiddish
3 Familiar joke, with "an"
4 Coleridge work
5 Average, to 11-Down
6 Spreadable cheese
7 Czar or king
8 Word after political or party
9 "Tut-tut"
10 Iota
11 World Golf Hall of Famer Isao ___
12 Proofer's mark
13 Anger
18 Calif. setting for *Stand and Deliver*
20 "We hold these ___ to be self-evident ..."
23 Enters the picture
24 Line-___ veto
26 Variety of poker

28 Get done
30 Sailor, slangily
31 Miss a cue
32 Spanish king
34 Detective
36 Came down with
37 NYSE debut stock
38 Nov. 11 honoree
39 Heretofore

40 Jared of *Dallas Buyers Club*
44 Peyote
46 Throws
47 President Harding's nickname
48 Sprinkle oil on
49 Actress Zellweger
51 Action film highlight

53 Slip on the galley
54 Existing
55 ___ of Man
57 Lay down some chips
60 Employee of Santa
61 Either Pres. Bush
62 Travel guide listing

SIX IN A ROW

ACROSS

1 Airline founded in 1927
6 Rutherford B. Hayes, astrologically
11 Health resort
14 Letter before iota
15 Atlantic or Pacific
16 1960s White House beagle
17 Woodcutter
18 She liked CB radios and mood rings
20 "Hurrah!"
21 David McCullough's *Truman*, e.g.
22 Roughly
23 She was inducted into the National Women's Hall of Fame in 2002
27 Hard to upset
28 Branch
29 Suffix with beat or neat
30 She launched the "Just Say No" campaign
37 Googol starter
38 Show displeasure
39 "Evil Woman" rock group
40 She established a foundation for family literacy
46 "___ Buck" (President Buchanan's nickname)
47 Tempe sch.
48 Eucalyptus-eating animals
50 She holds a postgraduate degree from Yale
56 Oklahoma Indian
57 Tic-tac-toe line
58 Unit of gunpowder
59 She was once a second-grade teacher in Texas
62 Cheese product?
65 Golfer Ernie
66 Must, slangily
67 Cathedral recesses
68 Easter purchase
69 ___ *Frome*
70 Carries

DOWN

1 Quart divs.
2 Shout of inspiration
3 Either President Roosevelt, e.g.
4 Relaxed
5 *Gilligan's Island* castaway
6 Advocacy group
7 Strand during a blizzard
8 Support, at the track
9 Fink
10 Unspecified number
11 Pint-sized
12 Intrinsically
13 Passion
19 Pro ___ session (short Senate meeting)
23 Spanish queen
24 Meadow
25 Jam ingredient?
26 "My lips ___ sealed"

27 Hoity-toity person
31 Celtics' org.
32 Corn holder
33 "That means ___!"
34 President Hoover's early occupation
35 Poe's middle name
36 Signs of approval
41 Haying machine
42 Drunk ___ skunk
43 Karel Čapek play
44 Hit the slopes
45 Warns, as a fellow driver
49 Resuming the previous speed, in music
50 Sank, as a putt
51 Europe's "boot"
52 No-good type
53 Leader of a hostel takeover?
54 ___ Rica
55 Lindsay of *Mean Girls*
60 35 is the minimum, for a U.S. president
61 Droid
63 American patriot "Light-Horse" Harry ___
64 Twisty turn

THE SAGE OF 61-ACROSS

ACROSS

1 Zealous
5 End-of-class signal
9 New York and New Orleans, e.g.
14 Boozy one
15 Brainstorm
16 Roger who wrote *Your Movie Sucks*
17 Makes mistakes
18 Labor-saving device developed by Thomas Jefferson
20 Turns right
22 Catty remark?
23 Battery for many penlights
24 Took the bait
25 With 39- and 52-Across, words from the Declaration of Independence, drafted by Jefferson
30 Burma's first prime minister
31 ___ Mae (*Ghost* role for Whoopi)
32 Garcia and Warhol
33 "What can I help you with?" asker
35 Stranded, as a ship
39 See 25-Across
43 Housekeeper's activity
44 Grandson of Adam
46 ___ Doone cookies
49 Lincoln center?
51 Furniture mover
52 See 25-Across
56 "___ Beso" (Paul Anka song)
57 Cheyenne's locale: Abbr.
58 ___, *amas, amat* ...
59 Huff and puff
61 Jefferson's home, a UNESCO World Heritage Site
66 Dance move
68 Fiery feeling
69 On
70 Bar mitzvah dance
71 Gets close to
72 Boy ___ door
73 Formerly, old-style

DOWN

1 Leave dumbstruck
2 Where 61-Across is
3 As payment
4 One tablespoon, e.g.
5 Auction action
6 Web address ending
7 "I wanna!"
8 Record company
9 Tiny brain size
10 Kimono sash
11 Slow down
12 Global agreement
13 Alley cats, maybe
19 President Wilson's conflict: Abbr.
21 ___-mo
24 Greyhound, e.g.
26 The 43rd state

27 Steely Dan singer Donald
28 Makes verboten
29 Provide
34 Tony winner Menzel
36 Campus in Troy, N.Y.
37 Postal scale marking
38 Yens
40 Sand ___ (golf hazard)
41 Jefferson, notably
42 Old bank giveaways
45 ___-Caps candy
46 One at the bottom of a totem pole
47 From way back when
48 Girl in a Beach Boys #1 hit song
50 Mind reader's skill: Abbr.
53 Lobbying gp.
54 "That is to say ..."
55 Jefferson portrayer in 1995's *Jefferson in Paris*
60 ___ Stadium (U.S. Open tennis venue)
62 Craggy peak
63 Org. that issues many refunds
64 Bagel topper
65 Make a pick
67 Butter slice

THREE LITTLE MONOGRAMS

ACROSS

1 Jacket fastener
5 "Pomp and Circumstance" composer
10 Federalist Webster
14 Capitol ___ (D.C. landmark)
15 Nary a soul
16 Land parcel
17 Jazz great Fitzgerald
18 Theodore Roosevelt's nickname, with "The"
20 Blue Cross rival
22 Flair
23 Termination
24 Place for bowlers?
27 Tiny amounts
29 "What ___ the odds?"
31 Sign before Virgo
32 *Portnoy's Complaint* author
34 Not decent
36 Henpeck
38 Parent, e.g.

42 Abraham Lincoln's first was on March 4, 1861
45 Matchbox racer
46 Ripen
47 1999 Ron Howard comedy
48 Yank or Ray
50 *Norma* ___
52 Cool, to a cat
53 Hunky-dory
56 Uzbek body of water
59 "Gotcha!"
60 Man, in Italy
62 Leaves port
65 Soviet leader who attended the 1945 Potsdam Conference with Harry S. Truman
69 Increase
70 Iowa college town
71 Ancient Greek theater
72 Mother of Helen, in myth
73 Edible seaweed
74 Out of style
75 Paradise

DOWN

1 Bygone Big Apple stadium
2 Aswan's river
3 2014 Tony-winning play about Lyndon B. Johnson
4 Main strategy
5 ___'acte (intermission)
6 President Hoover's wife
7 Attend, as a show
8 Reindeer's weapon
9 Singer McEntire
10 "Illmatic" rapper
11 Four duos
12 Political convention locale
13 Buffalo groups
19 American airline
21 The "A" in NATO: Abbr.
25 Term of office
26 Belly laugh
28 Major 19-Down hub

29 Came down
30 Clinton cabinet member Janet
33 Tough time
35 Like a certain nobleman's property
37 Festive affair
39 Like George Washington, as a boy
40 Ferrara ruling family
41 Invitation letters

43 Big name in political polls
44 Taj Mahal setting
49 Holiday Inn alternative
51 Skier's turn
53 Pat of *Wheel of Fortune*
54 "Yeah, you!" elicitor
55 Stand for a portrait
57 Cast openings

58 Bird on the U.S. presidential seal
61 "Come on now, that's enough!"
63 Prospector's discovery
64 Graceful bird
66 Clairvoyance, briefly
67 Aegean Sea island
68 L.A.-to-Butte direction

THE LION

ACROSS

1 *Mad Men* character Draper
4 Landlord's sign
9 Staff heads?
14 Inventor's cry
15 Puccini work
16 Tax cheat's risk
17 Rebellious Turner
18 Theodore Roosevelt, ideologically
20 Play about writer Capote
21 McKellen of *X-Men*
22 Modest knowledge
23 Cases for an otologist
26 Work at, as a trade
27 Tummy muscles
28 Hooters
30 Bashful
33 Like 35-Across
35 Canonized fifth-century pope
37 Light blue
38 Rainbow goddess
39 With 65-Across, toys named after Roosevelt
40 Roosevelt's ___ Moose Party of 1912
41 Minus
42 Not quite right
43 Do some yard work
44 Something to build on
45 Towel (off)
46 Tavern
47 Maya who designed the Vietnam Veterans Memorial
48 59-Across, e.g.
53 Points the finger at
57 Itinerary word
58 Hollywood ending?
59 Roosevelt's volunteer cavalry during the Spanish-American War
61 Clinton ___ (1993–2001)
62 *Tiny Alice* playwright
63 Three-card con
64 Commercials
65 See 39-Across
66 Bike routes
67 Cleaning substance

DOWN

1 Author of a classic translated into English by Calvin Coolidge
2 Scarlett of Tara
3 Roosevelt, notably
4 Debaters' needs
5 She dined with Barack on his 49th birthday
6 Sierra ___
7 Bit of energy
8 Pine products
9 Cellist Pablo
10 Full of passion
11 Cut and paste, say
12 Bill with Lincoln on it
13 Suffix with quip, hip, or tip
19 Puts to use
24 Chasm

25 Roosevelt, notably
29 Ties the knot
30 Roosevelt's domestic program
31 Burned-out ship, e.g.
32 President Taft's alma mater
33 San Juan ___ (site of a Roosevelt victory in 55-Down)

34 Creme-filled cookie
35 Woodworker, at times
36 Helper during crunch time
37 President James ___ Garfield
45 Well-formed thoughts?
46 Skewed views
47 Olympian sledder

49 Political fund-raiser, e.g.
50 Circumference
51 Dweebish
52 Flirtatious one
53 Emirate resident
54 ___ slaw
55 Spanish-American War battleground
56 Lamebrain
60 ___ good deed

IT'S GIVEN

ACROSS

1 President when women were first given the right to vote
8 Wanted poster items
15 Handle
16 President who wrote a biography of 1-Across
17 President who was the first to visit the People's Republic of China
18 Undying
19 Pep rally cry
20 Part of a geometric line: Abbr.
21 Radius, e.g.
22 Oklahoma city
24 With 38-Across, sushi fish
26 President who succeeded 17-Across
30 Longtime political gadfly Ralph
32 French artist Edgar

34 Noon, on a sundial
35 PC pop-ups
37 Baba ingredient
38 See 24-Across
39 How to answer the clues for this puzzle's ten presidents
43 Pros and ___
44 Go to seed
45 Melancholy
46 It may be inflated
47 Toys with tails
49 Bowling alley button
53 President when Medicare became law
55 Phoenix hoopster
57 Signal receiver
58 Hankering
60 "Bad call, ump!"
62 Old muscle car
63 "In case you didn't hear me ..."
66 President who debated Stephen Douglas seven times

68 President who was the last one from the Whig Party
69 Yachting event
70 Removes (oneself)
71 President who was victorious at the Battle of Shiloh

DOWN

1 President who succeeded 1-Across
2 Journalist Fallaci
3 Lady's-slipper, e.g.
4 Morse T
5 Genetic molecules
6 Fiends
7 Tightly packed
8 Starbuck's boss
9 Pastimes that use minifig avatars
10 Dunne and Cara
11 Better trained
12 Meet with
13 R.N. work areas
14 Aves.
23 Loved ones

25 Makes bubbly
27 Figure skating jump
28 Easter flower
29 Bad-mouth
31 Tpkes.
33 Chewing ___
36 Designs made from arrangements of thread
38 Wound up
39 Geezer
40 Informed about
41 "Ready or ___ ..."

42 Sculler's need
43 Cartoon collectible
47 ___ War (1950–53)
48 Outback manufacturer
50 Tourist attractions
51 Washington's Mount Vernon, e.g.
52 President who founded the University of Virginia

54 Having two parts
56 Prize won by three sitting presidents
59 LAX postings
61 Unrestrained romp
63 "___ Believer" (song written by Neil Diamond)
64 Tease
65 Chi-town rails
67 Smallish batteries

WAR HERO

ACROSS

1 Not more than
7 Political scandal of the early 1980s
13 General who allied with Dwight D. Eisenhower after D-Day
17 Eisenhower's 1948 memoir
18 Talk nonstop
19 Tabloid subject
20 Habitual drunk
21 Physicians' gp.
22 Atlanta-based TV network
24 Victorious general at Chancellorsville, 1863
26 General on a Chinese menu
27 Boring
32 Cotton bundle
35 Political platform?
37 Fourth down option
38 Lotion additive
39 Eisenhower's #2
40 Langston Hughes poem
41 Isn't able to
42 Unable to move
43 *Baseball Tonight* broadcaster
44 Parts of a system that grew during Eisenhower's presidency
46 RFK and others
48 Hive member
49 Stein filler
50 Perch in a church
53 A Gershwin
55 Reads, as a bar code
59 ___ blind eye (pretend not to see)
61 One of Eisenhower's longtime interests
64 Eisenhower rival in 1952 and 1956
65 Toadies
66 *Remington* ___ (Pierce Brosnan TV show)

DOWN

1 Capital of Ghana
2 Rhythmic humming sound
3 ___ Loa
4 About
5 Political biases
6 Kennedy or Cruz
7 Pulitzer-winning writer James
8 Cheap ornament
9 Big ___, California
10 Liquidation sales
11 Bowser's bowlful
12 TV's ___ *the Press*
14 Brief moments
15 It can be cast
16 Blowup: Abbr.
23 War zone during President Clinton's first term
25 Catches sight of
26 What tots do
27 Issue in many a presidential campaign

28 Inventor Sikorsky
29 Prom tux, usually
30 Alphabet quartet
31 007's school
32 Composer of *The Art of the Fugue*
33 Jai ___
34 Tape-measure home runs, e.g.
36 Itsy-bitsy
45 Certain terrier, informally
47 "Brace yourself"
49 1968 U.S. Open tennis champ
50 Plain writing
51 Sign up
52 Batman's alter ego
53 "If ___ be so bold ..."
54 Carnival attraction
56 Battle of Normandy city
57 "___ Poetica"
58 Big inits. in newspapers
60 ___ *Reader* (eclectic magazine)
62 "___ a Rock"
63 ER hookups

WHITE HOUSE LETTERS

ACROSS
1 Artery implant
6 Poor grades
10 Fury
13 Feet, in zoology
14 Heath's role in 2005's *Brokeback Mountain*
16 Butterfly catcher
17 George Washington, politically
19 Small songbird
20 Nevada senator Harry
21 Slapstick comedy props
22 Memorable 2011 hurricane
24 Summer on the Seine
25 Monopoly card
26 Visionary sort
27 Bye holder
28 Parts of feet
31 Adjust, as a corsage
34 Knot
35 Egyptian deity
36 Muffs
37 Certain navel
39 GPS suggestions: Abbr.
40 Lighten up?
41 Clamor
42 Royal pains
43 Really wants
45 Poses
47 Dom Pedro's slain lover
48 Tolkien creatures
49 Very, very soft, in music
52 Allies (with)
54 ___-dieu (kneeling bench)
55 Foal's father
56 Legal ending
57 John F. Kennedy, fashionwise
60 *House of Incest* novelist
61 Like some coincidences
62 Construction areas
63 Blaster's purchase
64 Loading place
65 Group of three

DOWN
1 Cathedral topper
2 Precept
3 World War I hero Rickenbacker
4 Penury
5 Recipe amt.
6 Said no to
7 Broke off
8 Hydrocarbon suffixes
9 Covetousness, e.g.
10 Basketball for Obama and golf for Eisenhower, e.g.
11 Bridle part
12 Sermon ending?
15 Hangouts for hogs
18 Sport with lunges
23 Calls it a career
25 Bear's home
26 Guard Chris who played his entire career with the New York Giants
27 Chapel in Vatican City
28 Hour on a grandfather clock

29 Artist Mondrian

30 Radiator sound

31 Funny Foxx

32 1813's Battle of Lake ___

33 Oval Office occupant (whose letters comprise every answer in this puzzle)

34 Former name of the cable channel Spike

37 Mid-March date

38 ___ for Noose (Sue Grafton novel)

42 Scoreboard nos.

44 Remainder, in Rouen

45 More insinuating

46 Social endings?

48 Els on a golf course

49 ___ Palace (Florence landmark)

50 Primp

51 As such

52 Transmitted

53 "Beauty ___ the eye of the beholder"

54 Gilpin of Frasier

55 Hubbub

58 Either Pres. Bush, e.g.

59 Round fig.

Answer, page 92

THE GREAT COMMUNICATOR

ACROSS

1 Sentry's order
5 Stucco backing
10 Snatch
14 Healthful berry
15 Hit that's not well-hit
16 Silver State city
17 Yanks' Civil War foes
18 Ronald Reagan's favorite snack
20 Plain English
22 Like Republican-leaning states
23 Peruvian range
24 With 57-Across, exclude
26 ___ firma
28 Silence
31 Corporate liabilities minus cash on hand
35 Big Apple sch.
36 Show-off in a show
38 Dam builder
39 Louis XIV, e.g.
40 U.S.-Soviet tensions that ended after Reagan's presidency

42 High dudgeon
43 *My Favorite Year* star, 1982
45 American Legion member
46 Pub draughts
47 Many Broadway performers
49 Doll party dishes
51 Director Welles
53 Svelte
54 Dressed up, on menus
57 See 24-Across
59 Colorado skiing mecca
62 1986 Reagan administration scandal
65 Verdi's slave girl
66 Chucklehead
67 ___ four (small cake)
68 ___ Curtain (symbol of the 40-Across)
69 Still-life pitcher
70 "Go ahead, ask"
71 Audition tape

DOWN

1 Heavenly strings
2 *Cars 2* henchman
3 Reagan headed one in the 1940s and 1950s
4 Like very thin paper
5 Prez who chose not to run for reelection
6 Oriole or Blue Jay, for short
7 For rent
8 Actor William, best man at Reagan's wedding to Nancy Davis
9 One who may bug you?
10 Island invaded in 1983 by U.S. forces
11 Peruse
12 Writer Rice
13 One calling the shots
19 Trade
21 Pipe joint
25 Mimics

27 Marketing come-ons

28 Seafood entree

29 Targeted amount

30 Prince of Broadway

32 What Reagan called the Soviet Union, in a 1983 speech

33 Special Forces cap

34 Long lock

37 Early 16th-century year

40 Church official

41 Freshly painted

44 First female Supreme Court justice, appointed by Reagan in 1989

46 "Let me repeat ..."

48 Later alternative?

50 Chicken ___ king

52 Harebrained

54 Taunt

55 Lined up

56 Tear down

58 In good shape

60 Land of Esau's descendants

61 Prefix with second

63 Select

64 Really enjoyed, with "up"

JUST THE FACTS, TOO

ACROSS
1 See 1-Down
4 Even though
10 "Whoops!"
14 Ingested
15 1957 hit for Jimmy Dorsey
16 Hand over
17 Hoedown partner
18 Furniture piece invented by Thomas Jefferson
20 Prohibition ___
21 Electronically scored duel
22 Missed the mark
23 With 50-Across, what Congress made George Washington posthumously in 1976
25 Choral work
27 "Gangnam Style" rapper
28 Emcee's need
29 Consumer protection org.
32 Ocean predator
35 Like some eclipses

36 It surrounds a 44-Across
37 President who, as secretary of state, actually drafted the Monroe Doctrine
41 Public house offering
42 Loosen
43 Red state in every presidential election since 1968
44 Spot in *la mer*
45 Fateful day
46 37-Across, to the second president
48 Relish
50 See 23-Across
54 Minos's land
56 Back into a corner
57 Taking after
58 Poet who read one of his works at John F. Kennedy's 1961 inauguration
61 *Great Expectations* boy

62 Wedding exchange
63 Blue blood, for short
64 "___ party time!"
65 ___ message
66 Includes as an extra
67 Buck's mate

DOWN
1 With 1-Across, fights big-time
2 Tempest game maker
3 Chill out
4 They may be fixed
5 Reason for unionizing, often
6 Prickly plant
7 Roof part
8 Dudgeon
9 ___ Aviv
10 Earthy colour
11 Symbol of life
12 Cartoon canine
13 Rustler's target
19 Et ___
24 Bridge
25 Chop up

26 Give a thumbs-up
28 Tax-exempt bonds, briefly
30 Tuscaloosa team, to fans
31 Big name in Texas politics
32 City near Santa Barbara
33 Hot dog holder
34 Swiss container?
35 Midsized soda bottle
38 Tremble
39 Reverse
40 Buggy place?
46 Takes care of
47 2,000 pounds
49 Secret event of 1945
50 "That's disgusting!"
51 ___ City (South Dakota city known as the "City of Presidents")
52 Supreme Court justice appointed by George W. Bush
53 Run out
54 Lit ___ (college course, slangily)
55 Took transportation
56 H.S. math class
59 Tit for ___
60 Man in a monastery

NAME TAGS

ACROSS

1 Pound sounds
5 Highlander, e.g.
9 Pasta shape
14 Noted LBJ biographer Robert
15 Evil Norse god
16 Harry Truman played it
17 Abraham Lincoln's nickname
20 "___ the Beautiful"
21 Paisley or plaid
22 Eight furlongs
23 Step on it
24 Dashboard display
26 Tolkien creature
27 Los Angeles's San ___ Bay
31 "___-daisy!"
32 Wash (out)
34 Part of ETO: Abbr.
35 Confucian principle
36 "___ Fox of Kinderhook" (Martin Van Buren's nickname)
37 Anti votes
38 George W. Bush is the only president with one
39 Org. that covers the White House
40 Pulsating
42 Swelter
43 ___ a clue (is lost)
45 Sculpting medium
46 Eats like a bird
47 Soap opera character Kane played by Susan Lucci
49 Toothed part
50 Perennial loser
53 Bach choral piece
56 Woodrow Wilson's nickname
58 Davis of *Jungle Fever*
59 One of 132 in the White House
60 Chinese dynasty
61 Jabs
62 Eastern discipline
63 Hip-hop wear designer Marc

DOWN

1 Official proceedings
2 Former Clinton advisor Emanuel
3 Fraternal group that included Washington and Truman
4 With regret
5 Pie piece
6 Fizzy drink
7 Approvals
8 William Henry Harrison's nickname
9 Closing statements?
10 "___ Jemmy" (James Madison's nickname)
11 Diminish
12 Lollapalooza
13 No longer new
18 Has the bug, say
19 Boy
23 Historic lead-in

24 Ronald Reagan's nickname
25 Bygone toothpaste brand
26 Andrew Jackson's nickname
28 Like a blue state
29 1980s craze starter
30 Ph.D. hurdles
32 Put chips in a pot

33 Male swan
36 Frenzied routines
41 HDTV brand
42 "No idea"
44 Fabled monster, informally
46 Former Clinton cabinet member Federico
48 "___ bin ein Berliner" (words from a Kennedy speech)

49 Beta follower
50 "Hold everything!"
51 "I get it now"
52 PC site
53 Thick-soled shoe
54 Popular road race
55 Movie set in Iran during Carter's presidency
57 Hugs, in a letter

DIAMOND LINKS

ACROSS

1 President who supported the Civil Rights Act of 1875
6 July 4, e.g.: Abbr.
9 Blue Ribbon brewer
14 Actress Perez
15 Email suffix
16 Sprinkle around
17 Baseball Hall of Famer Grover Cleveland ___
19 Rubbish
20 Pro vote
21 Forgo the script
23 Romeo's last words
24 Portrayer of 17-Across in a 1952 biopic
27 Not italic
30 Laid off
31 Baseball team for whom 24-Across recreated games as a radio announcer
36 Civil War side: Abbr.
39 West Wing worker
40 Meter reading
41 Some Ivy Leaguers
42 Urgent dispatch
43 Onetime 48-Across baseball team executive
45 Support beam
47 1960s–'70s radical Hoffman
48 See 43-Across
54 "Peanuts" expletive
55 "That's ___ shame"
56 Greedy one
59 Uneasy feeling
61 Slugger traded by 43-Across who later starred for the 31-Across
64 Get some shuteye
65 Cry at the World Cup
66 *Oklahoma!* aunt
67 *Steppenwolf* author
68 Flanders of *The Simpsons*
69 President nicknamed "His Accidency"

DOWN

1 Civil War side, with "the"
2 Credits listing
3 On the ocean blue
4 Cancel
5 Oolong, e.g.
6 Ibsen's Gabler
7 Newbery-winning author Scott ___
8 Like some tabloid headlines
9 Winter hrs. in L.A.
10 Pertaining to part of the heart
11 Group that makes contracts
12 Photo tone
13 Middle schooler, maybe
18 A Bobbsey twin
22 Graft receiver
24 Census form info
25 ___ whim
26 Reagan advisors Rollins and Meese

27 Some TVs
28 President Taft's home state
29 When Medicare became law and the Vietnam War escalated
32 Opposite of *paz*
33 Spanish bear
34 Lincoln or Ford
35 Australian shoe brand
37 Mexican accord?

38 1975 Wimbledon champ
41 Goes back
43 Type of barbecue grill
44 Revolutionary ___
46 Moistens in a kitchen
48 Rubbish
49 Philly footballer
50 Match play?
51 Author Zora ___ Hurston

52 Laid bets at a casino
53 Slippery ___
56 Determiner of which way the wind is blowing?
57 "Point taken"
58 *Dumb & Dumber* actress Teri
60 King Kong, for example
62 Still and all
63 Tricky

Answer, page 91

51

THE GREAT EMANCIPATOR

ACROSS

1 Sports car, for short
5 *The King and I* setting
9 Popular online magazine
14 Synthesizer pioneer Robert
15 Song from the musical *Fame*
16 Fundamental belief
17 Attorney general William who served under George H.W. Bush
18 Constitutional amendment, supported by Abraham Lincoln, that abolished slavery
20 Deep
22 Union side in the Civil War, slangily
23 The drink
24 Nolan Ryan, once
26 Coll. campus that houses George W. Bush's presidential library
28 Divided
30 Thurmond who ran for president in 1948
35 Forehead part
37 Part of a school's website name
39 Defaulter's loss
40 Con
41 Flexible Flyers, notably
43 Diner sign
44 Take off
45 Go one better than
46 "... and so dedicated, can long ___" (words from Lincoln's address at 65-Across)
48 ___ Theatre (where Lincoln was shot)
50 Frequent fliers?
52 Cuba's ___ of Pigs
53 Praline nut
55 Up to, informally
57 Civil War warship
61 Lab activity
65 Key Civil War battleground
67 Worshiped one
68 Lauder of cosmetics
69 Big furniture chain
70 Zola heroine
71 Political position
72 Have to have
73 From the top

DOWN

1 Prefix with dexterity
2 Advance
3 Site of the battle that started the Civil War
4 Feel the same
5 Looks after little ones
6 Ready to mate
7 "Thrilla in Manila" winner
8 Lincoln's wife
9 People in a pool
10 Onion's kin

11 Last of the Stuarts
12 French bean?
13 Biblical verb endings
19 Blacken
21 Catch red-handed
25 Popeye's "boy-kid"
26 Capitol Hill workers, say
27 ___ Park, New Jersey
29 Leaves home?

31 Trampled (on)
32 Lincoln, after 1854
33 Lincoln Center offering
34 Word with easy and even
36 ___ Piper
38 Functions
42 Lincoln's birthplace, famously
47 Clears after taxes
49 Neutered

51 Menu choice
54 Ambulance letters
56 1986 memoir by music's Turner
57 A long, long time
58 For fear that
59 Girl or boy lead-in
60 Bingo call
62 "Yikes!"
63 Zero
64 Chew (on)
66 Island strings

THE ONE AND ONLY

ACROSS

1 Point a finger at
6 K-5 sch. designation
10 Lincoln and others
14 Recluse
15 Pop
16 Popular teen hangout
17 Gerald Ford is the only president who was an ___
19 Where President Grant was born
20 Busy on the job
21 Cyclades island
22 Dial on the dash
24 William Howard Taft is the only president who later served on ___
29 Winter clock setting in Wash.
30 An avocation of Jimmy Carter and George W. Bush
31 Rabat's country: Abbr.
32 Was off base
36 Justice Dept. worker
37 Competent
38 Calvin Coolidge is the only president born on ___
42 Sword part
43 Reason for a tenth inning
44 Nigeria's capital before Abuja
45 Baptist leader?
46 Dandy
47 2001 Will Smith biopic
49 Jimmy Carter is the only president who, after leaving office, won a ___
56 Morales of *La Bamba*
57 Onetime comrade of Fidel
58 ESPN's Hershiser
59 Disney, for one
61 Franklin D. Roosevelt is the only president elected to ___
64 Dueling implement
65 High time?
66 They're verboten
67 Infirmary count
68 Urban problem
69 High point

DOWN

1 Sound from the fold
2 Not at all eager
3 1973 Rolling Stones hit
4 Goes soft
5 Poet's preposition
6 Debutante's date
7 Slack
8 Part of some email addresses
9 Have significance for
10 BP gas brand
11 Words from Scrooge
12 Gerald Ford, at law school
13 Traffic caution
18 Tastes
23 Civil Rights ___ of 1964

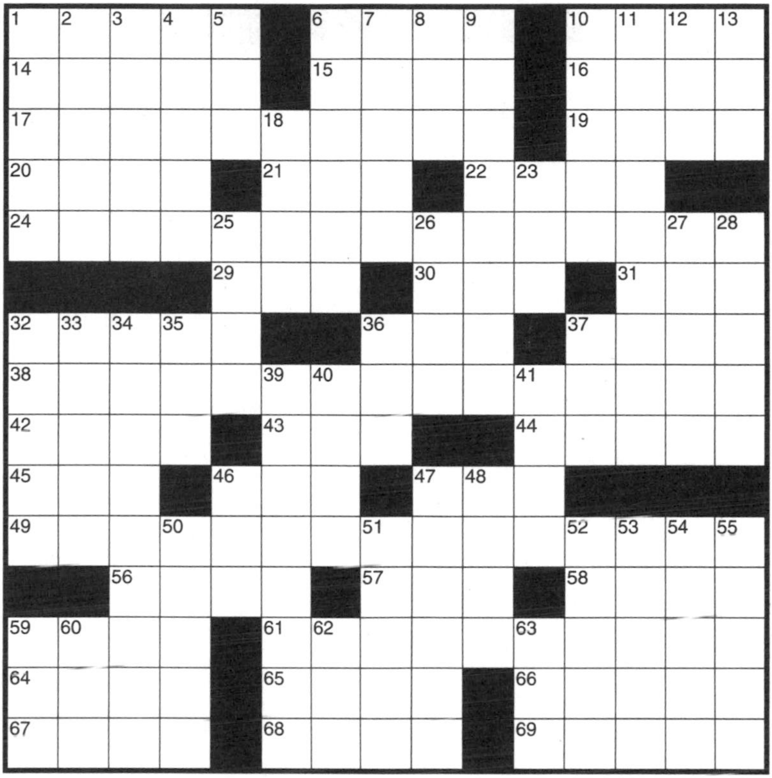

25 Prom hair style
26 Algebra class
27 Rich kid in "Nancy"
28 Deuce beaters
32 Patriot Allen
33 Safari sighting
34 Marked down for a sale, e.g.
35 Young newt
36 Snacked
37 Steely Dan double-platinum album
39 Idealists
40 Full-grown
41 Somersault
46 Contested state in the 2000 pres. election
47 In pain
48 Grouchoesque look
50 1956 vice-presidential candidate Kefauver
51 Sound before a blessing?
52 Helicopter part
53 *Me, Myself & ___* (2000 comedy)
54 Six in 1,000,000
55 Horror movie place, for short
59 Site for a site
60 Copy
62 Many a turkey
63 Political fund-raising org.

Answer, page 95

BUCK STOPPER

ACROSS
1 Treaty
5 See 56-Down
9 Harass nonstop
14 Wife of Jacob
15 Drivetrain part
16 Perfume quantity
17 *Je t'___* (French words of affection)
18 Harry S. Truman, for one
20 With 39-, 47- and 60-Across, comment attributed to Truman
22 Radio settings
23 Sample
24 Bar food?
25 Double curves
27 Site of Truman's presidential library
33 Dosage amt.
36 Scarf down
37 Whatsoever
38 "Go team!"
39 See 20-Across
42 Word with bag, ball, or caddy
43 Toothbrush brand
45 Prospector's find
46 Shortly
47 See 20-Across
51 Knocks for a loop
52 Poke fun at
56 Gave a bottle to
59 Top bond rating
60 See 20-Across
62 Weapon whose use Truman authorized at the end of World War II
65 Deborah of *Tea and Sympathy*
66 Like the sun god Inti
67 Noodle product?
68 1997 Peter Fonda title role
69 Croupiers' gear
70 Andrew Jackson's state: Abbr.
71 Annoying type

DOWN
1 Doesn't just warm the bench
2 Lawn tennis court set?
3 *The Fall* author Albert
4 Classic amusement park ride
5 Accurse
6 ___ ramp
7 Sharpton and Gore
8 *Gil Blas* writer
9 Male stay-at-home parent, familiarly
10 Sharer's word
11 Joule, e.g.
12 Birthplace of James K. Polk: Abbr.
13 Turn down
19 Gathering clouds, e.g.
21 Department of eastern France
25 Choices
26 Game-match connection
28 Cool, slangily
29 Musician's asset
30 Gp. that began during Truman's presidency

31 Disney goldfish
32 Dash or panache
33 *Star Trek* counselor Deanna ___
34 Hoedown site
35 Henry Higgins's creator
39 Doesn't cast a vote
40 Joule fraction
41 Capture
44 ___ Cruces, New Mexico

46 Advance unnoticed
48 Controversial govt. panel during Truman's presidency
49 Shortly
50 Giant Mel with 511 career home runs
53 One-named 2008 Grammy winner
54 Results of abrasion

55 Everglades wader
56 With 5-Across, Truman's domestic agenda
57 Highest European volcano
58 Place to tie one on?
60 FBI agents
61 Isracl's Abba
63 Sexy West
64 Words from Wordsworth

DOMESTICATED

ACROSS

1 Containing element #56
6 Cotillion honoree
9 Material for a coat?
14 Old Greek marketplace
15 Org. with a noted journal
16 Welcome to one's home
17 Summation
18 *Place for a second motorcycle rider* [Bill and Hillary Clinton]
20 *Old Nike ad campaign with all-around athlete Jackson* [Barack and Michelle Obama]
22 Heating option
23 One cause of weird weather
24 Yes, to Yvette
25 It may be bright
29 Presidential monogram
30 *Egg order* [Barack and Michelle Obama]
33 Creator of Atticus Finch
34 "And ___ you!" (answer to a name-caller)
35 First word of the answer to each of the six italicized clues
42 Column style
43 Some batteries
44 *It may affect one's fate* [Ronald and Nancy Reagan]
48 ___ moment
51 Grateful Dead founding member Phil
52 Barley wine, really
53 Actor Keanu
55 Frank McCourt memoir
56 *Mocking description of a self-important woman* [Lyndon and Lady Bird Johnson]
57 *Brit's afternoon refreshment* [George W. and Laura Bush]
62 "Do ___?"
63 War zone during Truman's presidency
64 Make a misstep
65 Obama's first secretary of defense
66 Change, as a will
67 Strike
68 Worries

DOWN

1 ___ wire fence
2 Ancient
3 Fabled Notre Dame football coach
4 Farsi speaker
5 Poultry choices
6 Small amounts
7 Big bird
8 Villain
9 Is profitable
10 Fool
11 29-Across, to voters
12 Actress Vardalos
13 Block buster?
19 Setting for an inaugural address

The grid contains numbered cells: 1, 2, 3, 4, 5, 6, 7, 8, 9, 10, 11, 12, 13, 14, 15, 16, 17, 18, 19, 20, 21, 22, 23, 24, 25, 26, 27, 28, 29, 30, 31, 32, 33, 34, 35, 36, 37, 38, 39, 40, 41, 42, 43, 44, 45, 46, 47, 48, 49, 50, 51, 52, 53, 54, 55, 56, 57, 58, 59, 60, 61, 62, 63, 64, 65, 66, 67, 68.

21 "___ you?"
24 What Drake and Pink are known by
25 Taylor Swift, e.g.
26 No more
27 Franc replacement
28 Take down ___
31 Originally
32 "Life ___ beach"
35 Wet blanket
36 Don Juan, for example
37 Letter attachments: Abbr.
38 Many a turban wearer
39 Unfriendly
40 Pick-up at a bar?
41 Rhone feeder
45 Babe in the woods
46 Loose overcoat
47 Hoists again, as sails
48 Do the Wright thing?
49 Origin of the word "Sabbath"
50 Take stock of
54 Conclude by
55 Loathsome one
56 47-stringed instrument
57 Cousin of reggae
58 Short canine, for short
59 Stuff to dig up
60 Tyler, in the presidential history books
61 Pitcher's stat

FATHERS AND SONS

ACROSS

1 Ex-president who swore in Hoover
5 Mexican peninsula
9 "It is a ___ day" (comment by John Adams before he died)
14 Over again
15 Mideast carrier
16 Unearthly
17 See 73-Across
18 It fell during George H.W. Bush's presidency
20 Raring to go
22 2013 Best Picture nominee
23 *Donnie* ___ (2001 cult movie)
25 Little visitor to Oz
28 New stock issuances, briefly
32 Eliminated, in a way
34 Crowning achievement
36 Role in *The Crying Game*
37 Four-door car, often
39 Shunned one
40 Six-Day War weapon
41 State acquired in 1821 by then–secretary of state John Quincy Adams
43 Thurman of *Kill Bill*
44 ___ Mesa, California
46 Item kept by John Quincy Adams
47 Back talk
48 Starts, as a journey
50 Albania's capital city
52 Back talk
53 Biblical twin
55 Studious group
56 Make "it"
58 Israeli desert
60 Law enacted during George W. Bush's first term, colloquially
65 "Livin' La Vida ___"
68 Not silently
69 Border on
70 "How sweet ___!"
71 "Care to?"
72 Second in a series
73 With 17-Across, occasional sea current

DOWN

1 Bit of ink, for short
2 *Wheel of Fortune* request
3 John Adams and others
4 Adjusts
5 Neuwirth on Broadway
6 On one's toes
7 Candy holder
8 ___ *the President's Men*
9 1968 presidential hopeful McCarthy, familiarly
10 New draft
11 Timeline segment
12 Feel bad
13 Business card abbr.
19 Denny's competitor

21 Succeeds big-time
23 Infers
24 State with 11 Electoral College votes
26 Simple wind instrument
27 Actress Raymonde of *Lost*
29 What George W. Bush and John Quincy Adams both lost once
30 In total agreement, with "of"
31 Colorful shawls
33 ___ Rio, Texas
35 Knocking off
38 Dummies
42 Richard Gere title role
45 Trial
49 Western lily
51 Land, as a fish
54 Full-length
57 Opera that premiered in Cairo
59 Jazzy James
60 Manhandle
61 Like
62 Quantity of bricks
63 Keyboard key
64 Prez on a fin
66 Org. once headed by George H.W. Bush
67 It bit Cleopatra

Answer, page 91

FOLLOW THE LEADER

ACROSS
1 Oversedated, maybe
6 Home of seven presidents
10 Turncoat
13 Broadcasting sign
14 La Scala cheer
15 Act humanly
16 Industrialist who introduced the Model T auto?
18 President Taft, at college
19 Fiendish
20 Mental flash
21 34th U.S. pres.
23 *Midnight in Paris* costar?
26 Changes the boundaries of
28 Exactly
29 Tag sale warning
30 Fake chocolate
33 "The King of Pop"?
40 Time out?
41 Kelly of morning TV
42 Tack on
46 Easter ___
48 *Sex and the City* actress?
52 "Fancy that!"
53 Burn application
54 Mocked
56 The Tigers, on an A.L. scoreboard
57 Noted women's retailer?
61 Red state?
62 Baseball Hall of Famer George
63 Sty cries
64 Blockhead
65 "No prob"
66 Old Palm smartphones

DOWN
1 Play-___
2 Washington bill
3 Universal
4 County Cork's country
5 Dust collector
6 With 7-Down, 2000 would-be presidential candidate
7 See 6-Down
8 "___ got it!"
9 Stick in the water
10 Further amend
11 Actress Dahl
12 Field hospital procedure
14 Ruin
17 Bossy types?
20 Hells Canyon locale: Abbr.
21 Pharmacist's weight
22 He loved Lucy
24 Gobs and gobs
25 LBJ in-law Charles ___
27 Bat wood
30 Cavs, on a scoreboard
31 Washington in D.C., e.g.
32 50 Cent's genre
34 *The Nazarene* author Sholem
35 Like some textbooks
36 Mantel piece

37 Notes to pick up on?
38 Blunted blade
39 Political forecaster Silver
42 Maine's ___ National Park
43 1840s White House family
44 Auctioned investments, briefly
45 Packed away
46 Composer Jacques
47 99 shares of stock, say
49 ___ of God (Jane Fonda movie)
50 Grant money?
51 Bye lines?
55 *The Kite Runner* boy
57 Mount Rushmore neighbor of Teddy
58 Org. that included Presidents Taft and Reagan
59 *Citizen Kane* studio
60 Head of state?

Answer, page 93

ARM-TWISTER

ACROSS

1 Crow's cry
4 "The magic word"
10 They may have jets
14 French agreement?
15 Site of Lyndon B. Johnson's swearing-in on 11/22/63
17 Part of TGIF
18 Policy liberalized in 1965 by Johnson-supported legislation
19 Adversary
20 Grazing area
21 Either Pres. Roosevelt, once
22 Actress Peeples
23 Broadway debut of 1982
25 Epic poet's instrument
26 *The Closer* broadcaster
27 Eyebrow shape
28 Schnozz tip?
30 Running ___
31 41-Across program

36 Cutout to fill in
37 Sports car feature
41 Johnson's domestic program, with "the"
43 Neighbor of Cambodia
46 *The Addams Family* cousin
47 What will be
48 Chemical suffix
49 Queens stadium
52 ___ worship
53 Robert Morse theater role
54 Flapper wrapper
55 Middle of a simile
57 Longtime NBA nickname
59 Subject of major legislation enacted during Johnson's presidency
62 Lennon's love
63 He received the first Medicare card from Johnson

64 Fly catcher
65 Supermodel Sastre
66 Say with conviction
67 Where both Roosevelts served as 21-Across

DOWN

1 Hairdo
2 Absolute ruler
3 Know-it-all
4 Some sand castle molds
5 Flavor in 7-Up
6 Humorist Bombeck
7 Movie org. with a Life Achievement Award
8 Saturated
9 Calculator message
10 TV ___
11 Start of an itinerary
12 Formally name
13 Where Nixon served before becoming vice president

64

16 Spelunking site
24 Some beachwear
25 W.C.
27 Reactions to cute babies
28 Mayberry boy
29 Showgirl in the song "Copacabana"
30 2004 Bill Clinton autobiography
32 Big ATM maker

33 Lead-in to while
34 Cheer (for)
35 Special treatment, for short
38 Try harder
39 Bill or Hillary Clinton, after Yale
40 End of a Salinger title
42 Draw
43 Chinese nut
44 TV's Monk

45 Body of work
49 Without messing up
50 In a way, slangily
51 Parts of locks
52 Lacks
55 Woeful words
56 Top banana
58 Perennial presidential campaign issue
60 Agcy. with auditors
61 Gloomy guy

FIRSTS

ACROSS

1 Shudder, e.g.
6 They're sometimes named after presidents
11 Place to park
14 Chill-inducing
15 Become frantic with fear
16 Rock producer Brian
17 Woodrow Wilson was the first president to have a ___
20 Truckload
21 "Vamoose!"
22 Over
23 Harry S. Truman was the first president to recognize the ___
27 Nile slitherer
28 2012 presidential contender Pawlenty
29 Decrease
32 Bowling surface
35 Japanese dog
37 It may go after you
38 Dull shade
39 Ronald Reagan was the first president to appoint a Hispanic person to his ___
41 Call for help
42 Sorority letter
43 Word with sing or string
44 Tailors
45 Suds dispenser
46 Paper size: Abbr.
47 Fighting Tigers of the NCAA
49 Dwight D. Eisenhower was the first president to have a ___
56 Separated
58 Voyaging
59 Chew the fat
60 Franklin D. Roosevelt was the first president to broadcast a speech in a ___
64 Affordable Care ___
65 Like a good cake
66 Pam of *Jackie Brown*
67 Rob ___
68 Writer Buchanan and others
69 Sign of contempt

DOWN

1 Back-to-school mos.
2 He ran against Clinton in 1992 and 1996
3 Bowl
4 Family nickname
5 Pickles
6 *Saturday Night Live* bit
7 Red River city
8 Like Brahms's Symphony No. 3
9 Chart shape
10 Loudly berate
11 U.S. aid program in World War II
12 In the past
13 Pointy-___
18 Hatchet job?
19 Lansing-to-Flint dir.

24 Trench coat color
25 Undercover operation
26 It's a tradition
30 It may be wiped
31 President Truman's wife
32 Deficiency
33 King Arthur of tennis
34 Lincoln's early political affiliation

35 End early
36 Blood
39 Signal a break in the action
40 Choir part
44 Good name for a trial lawyer
47 Bank holding
48 "Lowdown" singer Boz
50 Feeling of rage
51 Chip dip
52 Future attys.' hurdles

53 Marsh of detective fiction
54 Lyricist Carole Bayer ___
55 Roger who won a Pulitzer
56 Way off
57 Somewhat, musically
61 Word on U.S. currency
62 *Delta of Venus* author
63 Big coffeepot

GROANERS

ACROSS

1 First-time White House visitor in 1979
5 Flirted (with)
10 Dessert wine
14 Play ___ of tennis
15 Over
16 ___ B (alternative)
17 One of the Waughs
18 President's unseen purchase?
20 It may be skipped
21 Get better
22 Runs off
23 Stick ___
25 Retirement nest egg, briefly
26 Combining a president's deposits to prevent overdrafts?
34 Easter ___ roll (annual White House event)
35 "Is that so?"
36 Early course
37 Russia's ___ Republic
39 Once called
40 Film noir, e.g.
41 Twelve, maybe
42 Presidential inauguration event
44 Make a bow
45 John Donne line about a president?
48 Cured salmon
49 Dead waters
50 Hard wear?
53 ___ v. Ashcroft (2004 privacy case)
56 Large number
59 President's sci-fi weapon emissions?
61 Construction piece
62 Computer offering
63 Quick-footed
64 Inkling
65 Terrier type
66 Fit
67 Seductive

DOWN

1 "I kid you not" TV host
2 ___ Accords (1993 agreement signed at the White House)
3 Voyeur
4 Blah, blah, blah: Abbr.
5 Blast furnace opening
6 Theater award
7 Health club class
8 Malevolent
9 Opium ___
10 Music appreciation?
11 Apricot relative
12 Tall story
13 Signs
19 Obama hairstyle, once
24 Famous Amos
25 Distant
26 Singer Rimes
27 White house?
28 Some sitters

29 Discontinued Olds model
30 Drug-free
31 Like some income
32 2006 Winter Olympics city
33 ___ demon
38 One that's similar
40 Exploit
42 Photos, slangily

43 Neglected
46 Nickelodeon explorer
47 Oscar Hammerstein's forte
50 Shipment to Iran during the Iran-contra affair
51 Raise a stink?
52 Loads of

53 Ship of myth
54 2012 presidential hopeful Herman
55 Fictional crocodile
57 Not real
58 Low part of a hand, maybe
60 Writer Hentoff

Answer, page 89

AN IMPORTANT DETAIL

ACROSS

1 Word with credit or debit
5 Church official ... or President Carter's 39-Down
11 Biblical mount
14 Stead
15 Yankee rival
16 Meditation subject
17 Cube creator Rubik
18 Forest canine ... or President George H.W. Bush's 39-Down
20 Sierra Nevada, for one
21 Prefix with pod
22 Breakfast item
23 Stack, in a way
24 Gives a lift
27 Deck officer
28 Protects, in a way
30 Drinking glass ... or President George W. Bush's 39-Down

32 Fix up
33 Keep in
34 Federal agency that uses the 39-Downs in this puzzle
41 Go with it
42 *Brave New World* drug
44 Door opener ... or President Ford's 39-Down
48 Stray, maybe
51 Superstar
52 Jefferson's Monticello, for one
54 When to tour Tours?
55 Grinder
57 Pay for a hand
58 Goose egg
59 State capital ... or President Eisenhower's 39-Down
62 Political contest
63 Tony winner Cariou
64 More important
65 Wally of cookie fame
66 Mag. wheels

67 Hunts by tracking
68 Desires

DOWN

1 More easily understood
2 Fleet runners
3 Rebel ... or President Obama's 39-Down
4 Running mates, e.g.
5 "Let's hear it"
6 Author Jong and others
7 Set one's sights on
8 Ear part
9 ___ Miss
10 Unlikely party animal
11 Lacking a key
12 Greet the president, maybe
13 Less belligerent
19 Development site
21 Subpar mark
25 Kitchen addition

26 Litigant
29 Informal footwear
31 "___ Unplugged"
33 Dallas-to-Austin dir.
35 Ill-fated 1968 pres. contender
36 Gen. Robt. ___
37 Kites and the like
38 Lobby add-on?

39 See 34-Across
40 Symbol like :)
43 Perpetual
44 Sign of acne
45 Put on a pedestal
46 Wise lawgivers
47 Croat, e.g.
48 Cavalry member ... or President Kennedy's 39-Down

49 Web-footed mammals
50 Date
53 Dance that "takes two" to do
56 Barbecued dish
60 Slight downturn
61 ___ ideal
62 2004 biopic nominated for Best Picture

Answer, page 91

PRESIDENTUS INTERRUPTUS

ACROSS

1 Geisha's accessory
4 ___ of 1893 (economic event while Grover Cleveland was president)
9 Basketball Hall of Famer Baylor
14 Corporate VIP
15 One bit
16 Living ___
17 With 38- and 63-Across, a unique Cleveland presidential achievement
20 Dive in
21 Go after
22 Madison's home: Abbr.
23 Soft shoes
26 Make
29 Candy bar thought by some to be named for Cleveland's first child
33 Daily Planet worker Jimmy

34 Internet address suffix
35 Second edition
38 See 17-Across
44 Blackmailer, e.g.
45 2016 Olympics locale
46 Win, as a state in an election
49 President who defeated Cleveland in 1888, then lost to him in 1892
52 Fires up
55 Some whiskeys
56 Family-friendly movie ratings
57 Soccer stadium shout
59 Elegiac music
63 See 17-Across
68 With 60-Down, motorist's query
69 It's found under a tree
70 Carried out
71 Went wrong
72 Legend maker
73 Jimmy Carter's first naval rank: Abbr.

DOWN

1 Newspaperman Adolph
2 Symbol of redness
3 ___ caucuses (electoral event)
4 Leader of a flock
5 Fillmore, Pierce, or Coolidge, e.g.: Abbr.
6 "I'll pass"
7 Seine sights
8 Influence
9 Building wing
10 Ballad
11 Stomach sounds
12 Set off
13 Star of the *Taken* films
18 General assembly?
19 Prefix with natal
24 Behind the ___ (lagging)
25 Direct
27 Talk up
28 On the safe side

29 Track transaction
30 Commotion
31 Route follower
32 Snag
36 Testify in court
37 "My bad"
39 Hose color
40 Orbison and Rogers
41 Monopoly quartet: Abbr.

42 "O ___ babbino caro" (Puccini aria)
43 Heir, maybe
46 Chicago Outfit gangster
47 One before the Supreme Court
48 Play list?
50 It was divided in Exodus
51 Fertility goddess

53 Canon camera
54 Unsolicited manuscripts
58 Tunnel effect
60 See 68-Across
61 Enter
62 Objectives
64 Poetic praise
65 Rage
66 Pink-slip
67 Announcer Hall of *Merv Griffin's Crosswords*

QUICK QUIPS

ACROSS

1 Some sporty cars, informally
5 Olympic ___
10 Assns.
14 Medicinal plant
15 President who was editor of the Harvard Law Review
16 Chute opener?
17 Accumulation
18 "When the president does it, that means that it is ___": Nixon
20 Moreover
21 Break off
22 She outwitted Sherlock
23 "Read my lips, no ___": George H.W. Bush
25 Big spreads
26 Rest on
27 Lincoln's youngest son
28 Squelched
30 Lockup
32 Asia's ___ Sea

36 "Blessed are the young, for they shall inherit ___": Hoover
39 Play area
40 Black
41 Relieved
42 Census form info
43 Desktop buy
44 President who succeeded Garfield
48 "More and more of our imports come from ___": George W. Bush
52 Titter
53 White House ___ corps
54 Source of information for many policy decisions: Abbr.
55 "Forgive your enemies, but never forget ___": Kennedy
57 Short range?
58 Short notes
59 Wide open

60 Sleeper ___
61 Lincoln's profile is on it
62 Cliff-hanging
63 Actress Falco

DOWN

1 1940s Axis Powers member
2 Dior design
3 Johnson rival in 1964
4 "Get it?"
5 Follow
6 ___ it all
7 Blokes
8 Kuwaiti ruler
9 Danny's *Do the Right Thing* role
10 *Nixon in China*, e.g.
11 Furies
12 Victor in the Battle of Shiloh
13 Door-to-door work
19 Told stories
21 Hot spot
24 Long-term security, for short
25 FDR's dog

27 Peewee
28 Dump
29 "Oh, I see"
30 Throw curse words at?
31 Hunky-dory
32 Jefferson's predecessor
33 Showed admiration for
34 '60s White House nickname
35 Bygone Ford model
37 Stratum
38 Some jets
42 One who goes a-courting?
43 Tenant
44 Lofty story
45 Break new ground?
46 NYC landmark
47 Bank job
48 Financial adviser Suze
49 Prez backups
50 Garlicky mayonnaise
51 Black
53 Congressional worker
56 Athlete with a "W" on his cap
57 Top-notch

MASS. APPEAL

ACROSS

1 Watched
4 Girl in a #1 Everly Brothers hit
9 Hugo contemporary
14 Western native
15 Justice Kagan
16 Lexicon topic
17 Guitar great Paul
18 1960 John F. Kennedy campaign catchphrase
20 Corpulent
21 Two-time also-ran to DDE
22 Lozenge brand
23 Pete Rose had a record 14,053 of them
25 Bearded, as grain
26 Jeff Lynne's band, for short
27 Come in second
28 One of the Kardashians
31 Slip
33 Raison d'___
34 "Beat it!"
35 String tie
36 Hideouts
37 Tuscan river
38 "You wish!"
39 Height
40 Like this crossword
41 Kyoto cash
42 "There's not ___ bone in his body"
43 Pompous sort
44 Voting groups
45 President Ford, at birth
48 City west of Sherman Oaks
50 Number of Beethoven operas
51 Have a bawl
52 Program accelerated during Kennedy's presidency
54 1960s White House pet
55 Where Mocha is
56 Spaghetti sauce brand
57 Tip of a tongue?
58 Actions
59 Nursery rhyme eater
60 Check for accuracy

DOWN

1 Kind of drug
2 Troubled
3 Site of a memorable 1963 Kennedy speech
4 Kennedy, for eight years
5 ___ Gold (1997 movie)
6 Embroiders a bit
7 Foot soldiers: Abbr.
8 Chief Justice who swore in Kennedy on 1/20/61
9 Port on the Firth of Tay
10 You: Spanish
11 Key
12 For all ___ (G-rated)
13 Rev.'s address
19 Pound parts

24 Stuck-up
25 Some Nissan sedans
27 1961 Kennedy-supported volunteer program
28 Kennedy's adversary during the 1962 Cuban missile crisis
29 Actress Skye of *Say Anything ...*
30 Temper

31 Site that began as AuctionWeb
32 Kennedy family matriarch
34 Dance that came from Puerto Rico
36 *Sanford and Son* son
40 The Kennedy years, in the media
42 They're out of this world

44 Sent secretly by email: Abbr.
45 Europe's second-largest lake
46 Get up
47 Citi Field player, for short
48 Foil alternative
49 Handle
50 Finished
52 Barrett of Pink Floyd
53 Artist Jean

BEFORE ENTERING POLITICS

ACROSS

1 Fizzle, with "out"
6 President whose monogram is the same as those of his wife and daughters
9 ___-off (shortened)
14 Obliterate
15 Mentalist Geller
16 Resembling
17 Friendliness
18 With 60-Across, Barack Obama's onetime occupation
20 Green shade
21 Racket
22 2012 presidential campaign name
23 Start of a Spanish count
24 6-Across's onetime occupation
26 Women's ___
29 One-___ (politician with a short career)
31 On
33 Stylish suit
36 Largest of a septet
37 Warren Harding's onetime occupation
42 "Too bad"
43 Sports stats
44 Dessert wine
47 Wish "bon voyage!"
51 John Kerry, collegiately
52 Theodore Roosevelt's onetime occupation
55 Group that included JFK among its members
56 Unreactive element
58 Careless
59 Beverage enjoyed by Washington, Jefferson, and Obama
60 See 18-Across
63 Oregon city where Herbert Hoover grew up
64 Grace under fire
65 Attention
66 Blow away
67 Moderated, with "down"
68 Prohibitionist
69 VCR, e.g.

DOWN

1 With 50-Down, Jimmy Carter's onetime occupation
2 Fine fur
3 Andrew Johnson's onetime occupation
4 Old notable Italian family
5 Marina del ___, California
6 Donizetti's operatic bride
7 Rodeo ride
8 Huck Finn's pal
9 Pipsqueak
10 Spider-Man's ___ May
11 A college applicant may be on it
12 Superlative suffix

Down

13 Handyman's letters
19 Strasbourg ladies: Abbr.
21 Body layer
24 ACC athlete
25 They may be split
27 Peculiar: Prefix
28 Grizzly, e.g.
30 Pool shot
32 Union demand
34 "Sounds like ___"
35 Modern start?
37 Dog tag info
38 Company of Israeli bankers?
39 Attacking vigorously
40 Big-selling 1920s car
41 Some game
45 Pressed
46 Indian princess
48 Quarter-mile, maybe
49 Restraining order?
50 See 1-Down
53 Weather forecast
54 Follower of Franklin
57 Allay
59 Ole Miss rival
60 Go (for)
61 Piglet pal
62 Letter from London
63 Was idle

MAN OF HOPE

ACROSS

1 It may follow an intermission
7 ___ Simbel, Egypt
10 Canal sites
14 Consider again, in court
15 Gilbert & Sullivan operetta
17 Real
18 With 35- and 57-Across, 1992 27-Down campaign catchphrase
19 When Paris is burning?
20 Waits by a microphone
22 Inventor's monogram
23 Gilbert & Sullivan princess
24 Part of NAFTA
26 Clinches
28 Belgian balladeer
29 Drain
30 Where 27-Down went to law school

31 News gatherers
32 Certain sci. major
33 "___ wrong?"
34 The 27-Downs, e.g.
35 See 18-Across
40 A couple of Mexicans?
41 "Mazel ___!"
42 Bauhaus artist Paul
44 Put an edge on
47 Loser to 27-Down in 1996
48 Sight from Taormina
49 Clumsy ones
50 Ocean liner?
51 "Later"
52 Habitually, to poets
53 Opinion
54 1972 treaty subj.
56 Hosp. scan
57 See 18-Across
60 Not yet home
62 1979 hostage takers
63 Gauchos' gear

64 *Hairspray* role
65 Cut
66 Come after

DOWN

1 Light song
2 27-Down, ideologically
3 Carole King feels it move, in a song
4 Your, to Yves
5 It may be toxic
6 Three-layer snack
7 Foreign ___
8 Infant's shoe
9 Radii parallels
10 JFK's naval rank
11 Duds
12 Sponsor of 27-Down's scholarship to 45-Down
13 Floral components
16 Nibbled away
21 ___ Beach (site of both 1972 political conventions)

25 Mocks
27 #42 in the presidential history books
28 Put up with
30 Talks a blue streak
31 Dartboard setting
34 1993 movie about a presidential impersonator
36 Affirmative action?
37 Israel's Meir
38 Eventual
39 Instrument played by 27-Down
43 Least puzzling
44 Rock's ___ & the Blowfish
45 See 12-Down
46 Court figure
47 The start of something
50 President Polk's wife
51 Prenatal exam, for short
53 Mumbai Mr.
55 Five-time Wimbledon champ
58 ___ roll
59 Vane dir.
61 Preclusion

Answer, page 91

WHITE HOUSE PLOT

ACROSS

1 Dish (out)
5 Gulf
10 Impostor
14 Norwegian saint
15 Wasn't given a choice
16 Knocked off
17 White House area whose primary contents you can find nine times in this puzzle's completed grid, looking across, down, up, backward, and diagonally, word-search style
19 Frobe who played Goldfinger
20 Decide
21 Swell
22 Nicholas II, e.g.
24 Crystal ball gazers
26 Some getaway places
27 In ___ (actually)
28 Farm milk provider
30 Philosopher Kierkegaard
32 Like some wines
36 Shiba ___ (Japanese dog breed)
37 Regular events in the 17-Across
41 Roll call call
42 An operation might be given one
43 Wound up
45 Take the wrong way?
46 Outdoor cover
50 Court workers, for short
53 Famous Titanic victim
54 ___ Stone
55 Mo. that Lincoln and FDR died
57 Baja bear
58 Lover of Psyche
59 2006 Stanley Cup champs honored in the 17-Across
62 Artful
63 Web mag
64 "... a ___ which will live in infamy ...": FDR
65 About
66 Golf's ___ Cup
67 Turnstile feature

DOWN

1 Gloomy
2 Runs to Vegas, maybe
3 Predilections
4 Christmas ___
5 Labor secretary Elaine who served from George W. Bush's first day in office to his last
6 Christmas carol opener
7 Total
8 Cubic meter
9 Old hi-fi records
10 Operatic barber
11 Having no middle
12 Lantern filler
13 Ron Howard media satire

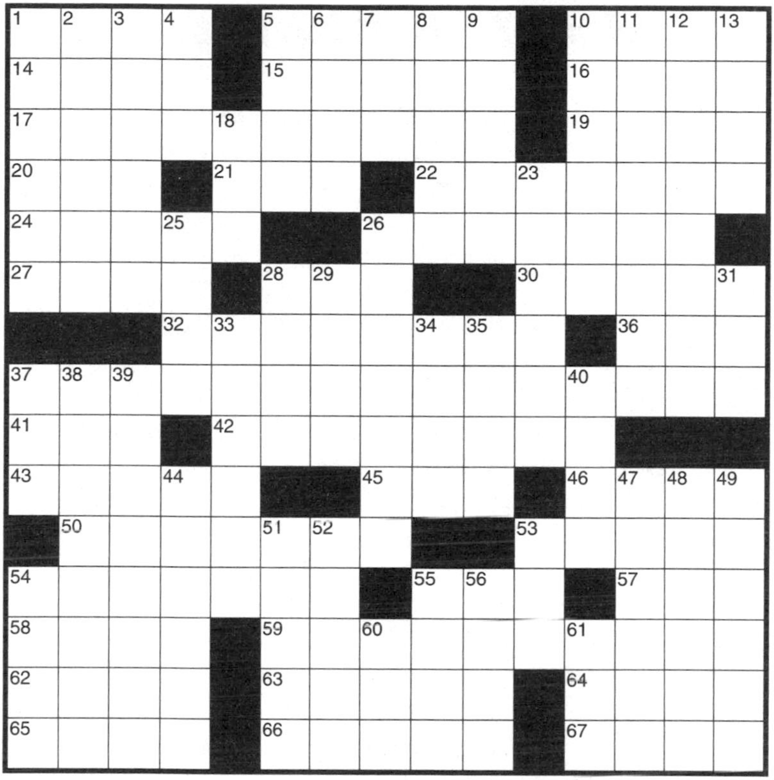

18 Empty talk
23 Like most 35-Downs: Var.
25 Guns
26 Joints
28 Switch finish?
29 Empty talk
31 Greek consonants
33 Sign of stress?
34 ___'clock scholar
35 Middle Easterner, perhaps
37 Member of a D.C. nine
38 Dumps
39 Got all mushy
40 Fishing aids
44 Is responsible for
47 Like much of Alban Berg's music
48 Met, as a challenge
49 Split backs formation, in football-speak
51 Additional
52 Transparently thin and light
53 Firecracker's trajectory
54 The scarlet letter
55 "Rule Britannia" composer
56 Place to get a bite?
60 Purge
61 Political campaign staples

Answer, page 93

MAKING HISTORY

ACROSS
1 Pantry problem
5 Polite terms of address
10 Threads
14 *Bush v.* ___ (2000 Supreme Court case)
15 Early Michael Caine role
16 Eye part
17 Something for trill-seekers?
18 More peeved
19 Mad Libs request
20 What 39-Across declined in his two presidential campaigns
23 Chemical ending
24 March org.?
25 See 38-Across
26 On a roll
27 Sorkin who created *The West Wing*
30 39-Across's #2
33 Memo intro
34 39-Across was its Person of the Year in 2008 and 2012
38 With 25-Across, numbers in parentheses
39 "No-drama" president
40 Wander
41 Don't Ask, Don't ___ Repeal Act of 2010
42 39-Across and others: Abbr.
43 Some 26-Down projections
44 Sampling
46 Part of USMA: Abbr.
47 *60 Minutes* regular
50 Laughfest
52 Any first lady
55 Where 39-Across used to teach constitutional law
59 *Il pontefice*'s home
60 Like a rainbow
61 Mitt Romney's wife and others
62 Junkie
63 Daft
64 Hummus holder
65 Eliot protagonist
66 Shaped (up)
67 Unhurried

DOWN
1 Obviously surprised
2 Like some stockings
3 Crow or Cree
4 Member of the Navy team that killed Osama bin Laden
5 Elephant or donkey, in politics
6 Up in the air
7 Like 39-Across but no other president
8 Bearing
9 Hospital supplies
10 Important issue to 39-Across
11 Don't touch
12 Get back together
13 Mamie Eisenhower's hairstyle

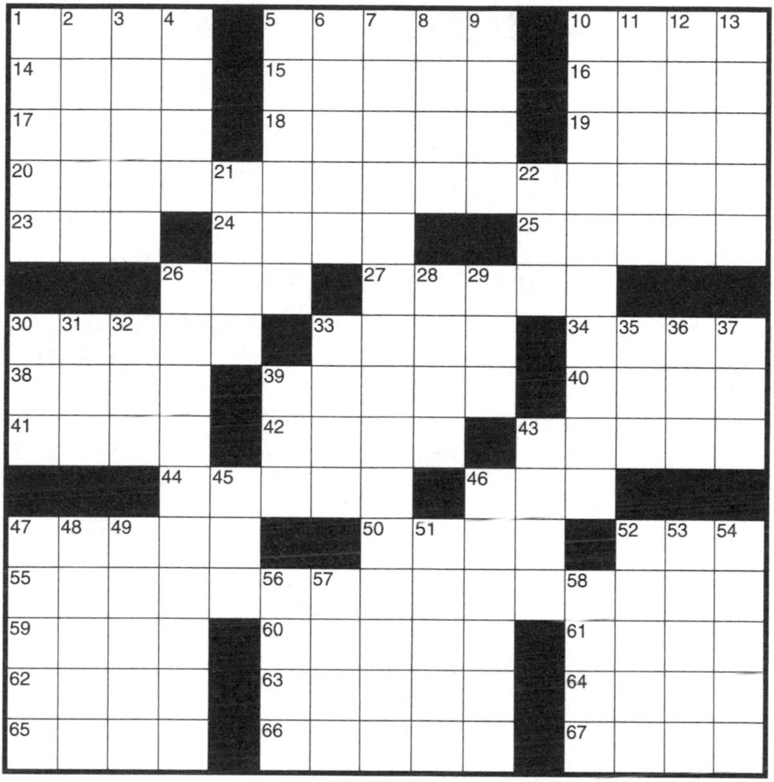

The crossword grid with numbered cells:

Row 1: 1, 2, 3, 4, [black], 5, 6, 7, 8, 9, [black], 10, 11, 12, 13
Row 2: 14, [black], 15, [black], 16
Row 3: 17, [black], 18, [black], 19
Row 4: 20, 21, [black], 22
Row 5: 23, [black], 24, [black], 25
Row 6: [black], 26, [black], 27, 28, 29, [black]
Row 7: 30, 31, 32, [black], 33, [black], 34, 35, 36, 37
Row 8: 38, [black], 39, [black], 40
Row 9: 41, [black], 42, [black], 43
Row 10: [black], 44, 45, [black], 46, [black]
Row 11: 47, 48, 49, [black], 50, 51, [black], 52, 53, 54
Row 12: 55, [black], 56, 57, [black], 58
Row 13: 59, [black], 60, [black], 61
Row 14: 62, [black], 63, [black], 64
Row 15: 65, [black], 66, [black], 67

21 It may be pumped
22 Barracks VIP
26 Important issue to 39-Across
28 Presidential coat of ___
29 Mens ___ (criminal intent)
30 Club for swingers?
31 Pique
32 30-Across's state: Abbr.
33 Sarcastic answer
35 Apple apps use it
36 Floor protector
37 Committee members?
39 Some ER cases
43 Field opening?
45 Where the Confederate flag was first flown: Abbr.
46 Worked by hand
47 Do away with
48 The others
49 Focused
51 Actress Graff
52 Supreme Court justice Sotomayor, a 39-Across appointee
53 Traces
54 Op-ed piece
56 Jog, say
57 Yes ___
58 Ponytail locale

Answer, page 95

6–7

C	H	A	L	K		S	A	N	G		O	P	E	D
H	A	S	O	N		A	B	O	O		N	O	S	E
A	L	I	F	E		W	E	A	N		E	L	S	A
S	T	A	T	E	O	F	T	H	E	U	N	I	O	N
M	E	G			L	U	I			A	F	I	T	
		D	O	M	E	S	T	I	C	P	O	L	I	C	Y
		A	R	T		W	O	E			C	U	E	
D	U	C	T	S		V	I	P		M	A	S	T	S
A	S	H			P	A	S		S	A	L			
H	A	I	L	T	O	T	H	E	C	H	I	E	F	
		L	O	A	N		M	A	A		L	A	W	
E	X	E	C	U	T	I	V	E	B	R	A	N	C	H
L	E	A	K		I	N	O	N		A	L	I	T	O
A	N	N	E		A	C	I	D		J	U	N	O	S
L	A	S	T		C	A	D	S		A	M	O	R	E

16–17

A	R	C		E	A	S	E	D		L	A	L	A	W
H	A	H		S	M	O	R	E		O	C	A	L	A
E	D	U		P	E	A	R	L	H	A	R	B	O	R
A	I	R		R	N	S		T	U	N	E	O	U	T
D	O	C	K	E	D		N	A	M	E		R	D	S
			H	A	S	S	L	E		A	D	D		
R	E	I	N	S		E	W	A	N		A	R	A	B
K	E	L	S	O		F	D	R		S	N	O	R	E
O	L	L	A		S	T	E	M		T	N	O	T	E
			S	A	T		A	S	T	R	O	S		
U	M	A		L	O	L	L		A	E	N	E	A	S
N	A	T	A	L	I	E		O	N	S		V	E	T
P	U	B	L	I	C	W	O	R	K	S		E	R	A
E	R	A	S	E		I	S	S	U	E		L	I	T
G	A	T	O	S		S	T	O	P	S		T	E	E

26–27

S	A	S	S		R	E	L	I	C		I	P	A	D
O	R	A	L		E	V	I	T	E		D	R	N	O
O	T	T	O		F	A	L	S	E	T	E	E	T	H
T	H	E	W	O	R	D	I			O	A	T		
H	U	E		B	Y	E		E	A	R	L	O	B	E
E	R	N	I	E		R	A	D	I	O		R	O	E
			L	S	U		L	E	D		O	I	N	K
	V	A	L	E	N	T	I	N	E	S	D	A	Y	
A	I	L	S		B	I	C		D	E	E			
S	A	M		V	A	N	E	S		E	D	I	T	H
S	L	A	V	E	R	Y		P	A	T		C	R	U
		N	A	T		N	A	P	O	L	E	O	N	
O	V	A	L	O	F	F	I	C	E		A	B	U	T
N	I	C	E		L	I	N	E	R		M	O	P	E
E	A	S	T		O	B	E	Y	S		A	X	E	D

36–37

D	O	N		T	O	L	E	T		C	L	E	F	S
A	H	A		O	P	E	R	A		A	U	D	I	T
N	A	T		P	R	O	G	R	E	S	S	I	V	E
T	R	U		I	A	N		S	M	A	T	T	E	R
E	A	R	A	C	H	E	S		P	L	Y			
			A	B	S		O	W	L	S		S	H	Y
H	O	L	Y		S	T	L	E	O		A	Q	U	A
I	R	I	S		T	E	D	D	Y		B	U	L	L
L	E	S	S		A	M	I	S	S		R	A	K	E
L	O	T		W	I	P	E			B	A	R		
		L	I	N		R	E	G	I	M	E	N	T	
A	C	C	U	S	E	S		V	I	A		D	E	E
R	O	U	G	H	R	I	D	E	R	S		E	R	A
A	L	B	E	E		M	O	N	T	E		A	D	S
B	E	A	R	S		P	A	T	H	S		L	Y	E

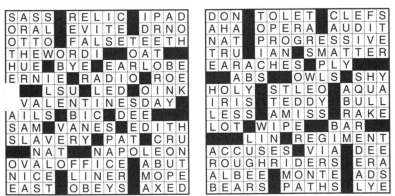

86

46–47

```
WAR   ALBEIT   OHOH
ATE   SORARE   CEDE
GAL   SWIVELCHAIR
ERA   EPEE   ERRED
SIXSTAR   MOTET
   PSY   MIKE   BBB
ORCA   LUNAR   EAU
JOHNQUINCYADAMS
ALE   UNTIE   UTAH
ILE   IDES   SON
   SAVOR   GENERAL
CRETE   TREE   ALA
ROBERTFROST   PIP
IDOS   ARISTO   ITS
TEXT   TAGSON   DOE
```

56–57

```
PACT   DEAL   HOUND
LEAH   AXLE   OUNCE
AIME   MISSOURIAN
YOUWANT   AMS   TRY
SUSHI   OGEES
   INDEPENDENCE
TBSP   EAT   ATALL
RAH   AFRIEND   TEA
ORALB   ORE   SOON
INWASHINGTON
   STUNS   TEASE
FED   AAA   GETADOG
ATOMICBOMB   KERR
INCAN   IDEA   ULEE
RAKES   TENN   PEST
```

66–67

```
SPASM   SHIPS   LOT
EERIE   PANIC   ENO
PRESSCONFERENCE
TON   SHOO   ENDED
STATEOFISRAEL
   ASP   TIM   EBB
LAWN   AKITA   ARE
ASH   CABINET   SOS
CHI   ALONG   SEWS
KEG   LTR   LSU
   PILOTSLICENSE
APART   ASEA   GAB
FOREIGNLANGUAGE
ACT   MOIST   GRIER
ROY   EDNAS   SNORT
```

76–77

```
SAW   SUSIE   DUMAS
UTE   ELENA   USAGE
LES   NEWFRONTIER
FAT   AES   LUDENS
ATBATS   AWNED
   ELO   PLACE   KIM
ERROR   ETRE   SHOO
BOLO   LAIRS   ARNO
ASIF   ACME   CLUED
YEN   AMEAN   ASS
   BLOCS   OMAHAN
ENCINO   ONE   CRY
SPACETRAVEL   HIM
YEMEN   PREGO   ESE
DEEDS   SPRAT   VET
```

8–9

L	I	M	A		C	E	D	E	D		S	H	A	H
A	L	A	S		A	R	E	N	A		C	A	P	A
B	E	R	T		B	R	I	T	I	S	H	S	P	Y
		K	O	I		C	O	R	E		A	L	E	
P	C	T		F	I	V	E	M	I	N	U	T	E	S
L	O	W	T	I	D	E		B	E	A	N			
A	B	A	R		O	N	S		S	T	E	P	P	E
T	R	I	A	D		D	O	N		E	A	R	E	D
T	A	N	D	E	M		B	O	A		S	E	R	E
			E	L	I	S		U	R	G	E	S	O	N
O	N	E	S	E	N	T	E	N	C	E		I	T	S
B	A	L		T	I	E	R			L	E	D		
A	G	E	S	E	V	E	N	T	Y		R	E	S	T
M	A	C	K		A	L	I	K	E		A	N	T	E
A	T	T	Y		N	Y	E	T	S		S	T	Y	X

18–19

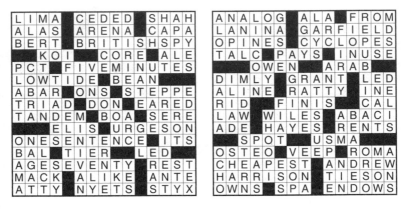

A	N	A	L	O	G		A	L	A		F	R	O	M
L	A	N	I	N	A		G	A	R	F	I	E	L	D
O	P	I	N	E	S		C	Y	C	L	O	P	E	S
T	A	L	C		P	A	Y	S		I	N	U	S	E
			O	W	E	N			A	R	A	B		
D	I	M	L	Y		G	R	A	N	T		L	E	D
A	L	I	N	E		R	A	T	T	Y		I	N	E
R	I	D		F	I	N	I	S			C	A	L	
L	A	W		W	I	L	E	S		A	B	A	C	I
A	D	E		H	A	Y	E	S		R	E	N	T	S
		S	P	O	T			U	S	M	A			
O	S	T	E	O		V	E	E	P		R	O	M	A
C	H	E	A	P	E	S	T		A	N	D	R	E	W
H	A	R	R	I	S	O	N		T	I	E	S	O	N
O	W	N	S		S	P	A		E	N	D	O	W	S

28–29

	S	N	O	O	P		B	R	A	T		W	A	S
W	O	U	L	D	A		R	U	N	S		H	O	T
R	O	D	D	E	R		I	L	I	K	E	I	K	E
A	T	N	O		T	E	E	M		A	T	I	T	
T	H	I	N	A	I	R		R	A	H	S			
H	E	K	E	P	T	U	S		L	I	T	T	E	R
			P	E	T	E	S		G	L	A	R	E	
G	I	V	E	E	M	H	E	L	L	H	A	R	R	Y
O	P	E	R	A		S	T	E	E	L				
T	O	T	E	R	M		O	U	T	O	F	W	A	R
		N	S	E	C		T	O	W	L	I	N	E	
T	R	I	O		S	H	A	H		I	N	O	N	
Y	E	S	W	E	C	A	N		G	I	N	N	I	E
P	A	L		L	A	S	T		E	N	G	I	N	E
O	L	E		F	L	E	E		O	N	S	E	T	

38–39

W	O	O	D	R	O	W		A	L	I	A	S	E	S
A	R	R	A	N	G	E		H	E	R	B	E	R	T
R	I	C	H	A	R	D		A	G	E	L	E	S	S
R	A	H		S	E	G		B	O	N	E			
E	N	I	D		S	E	A		G	E	R	A	L	D
N	A	D	E	R		D	E	G	A	S		X	I	I
			A	D	S		R	U	M		E	E	L	S
	F	I	R	S	T	N	A	M	E	O	N	L	Y	
C	O	N	S		R	O	T			S	A	D		
E	G	O		K	I	T	E	S		R	E	S	E	T
L	Y	N	D	O	N		S	U	N		D	I	S	H
			U	R	G	E		B	O	O		G	T	O
I	R	E	P	E	A	T		A	B	R	A	H	A	M
M	I	L	L	A	R	D		R	E	G	A	T	T	A
A	B	S	E	N	T	S		U	L	Y	S	S	E	S

88

```
A R F S   S C O T   E L B O W
C A R O   L O K I   P I A N O
T H E R A I L S P L I T T E R
A M E R I C A   P A T T E R N
    M I L E   P E D A L
D I A L S   O R C   P E D R O
U P S Y   B L E A C H   E U R
T A O   R E D   N O S   M B A
C N N   A T H R O B   B O I L
H A S N T   I C E   P E C K S
    E R I C A   G E A R
S A D S A C K   C A N T A T A
T H E S C H O O L M A S T E R
O S S I E   R O O M   M I N G
P O K E S   Y O G A   E C K O
```

```
B A R I C   D E B   P A I N T
A G O R A   A M A   A S K I N
R E C A P   B U D D Y S E A T
B O K N O W S   G A S
E L N I N O   O U I   I D E A
D D E   S U N N Y S I D E U P
    L E E   S O A R E
P R E S I D E N T I A L D O G
I O N I C   A A S
L U C K Y N U M B E R   A H A
L E S H   A L E   R E E V E S
    T I S   H E R N I B S
S P O T O F T E A   I D A R E
K O R E A   E R R   G A T E S
A M E N D   R A P   S T E W S
```

```
P O P E   T O Y E D   A S T I
A S E T   A B O V E   P L A N
A L E C   P I G I N A P O L K
R O P E   H E A L   F L E E S
    I T T O     I R A
L I N C O L N A C C O U N T S
E G G   R E A L L Y   S O U P
A L T A I   N E E   G E N R E
N O O N   P A R A D E   T I E
N O M A D I S O N I S L A N D
    L O X   S T Y X
A R M O R   A C L U   R A F T
R E A G A N R A Y S   I B A R
M E N U   A G I L E   C L U E
S K Y E   T O N E D   S E X Y
```

```
P E T E R   L B J   S A W E D
E R A S E   U R I   Q U A S I
A M I T Y   C O M M U N I T Y
N I L E   D I N   M I T T
U N O   T E A C H E R   L I B
T E R M E R   A S T R I D E
    A R M A N I   A S I A
N E W S P A P E R E D I T O R
A L A S   L O S S E S
M A D E I R A   S E E O F F
E L I   R A N C H E R   N R A
    N E O N   L A X   B E E R
O R G A N I Z E R   S A L E M
P O I S E   E A R   A M A Z E
T O N E D   D R Y   T A P E R
```

10–11

20–21

30–31

40–41

50–51

```
G R A N T ■ H O L ■ P A B S T
R O S I E ■ E D U ■ S T R E W
A L E X A N D E R ■ T R I P E
Y E A ■ ■ A D L I B ■ I D I E
■ ■ R O N A L D R E A G A N
R O M A N ■ ■ I D L E ■ ■ ■
C H I C A G O C U B S ■ C S A
A I D E ■ U S A G E ■ E L I S
S O S ■ G E O R G E W B U S H
■ I B A R ■ ■ ■ A B B I E
T E X A S R A N G E R S ■ ■
R A T S ■ A R E A L ■ P I G
A G I T A ■ S A M M Y S O S A
S L E E P ■ O L E ■ E L L E R
H E S S E ■ N E D ■ T Y L E R
```

60–61

```
T A F T ■ B A J A ■ G R E A T
A N E W ■ E L A L ■ E E R I E
T I D E ■ B E R L I N W A L L
■ ■ E A G E R ■ ■ H E R ■
D A R K O ■ T O T O ■ I P O S
E R A S E D ■ C A P S T O N E
D I L ■ S E D A N ■ L E P E R
U Z I ■ F L O R I D A ■ U M A
C O S T A ■ D I A R Y ■ L I P
E N T E R S O N ■ T I R A N E
S A S S ■ E S A U ■ N E R D S
■ ■ T A G ■ ■ N E G E V ■
P A T R I O T A C T ■ L O C A
A L O U D ■ A B U T ■ I T I S
W A N N A ■ B E T A ■ N E A P
```

70–71

```
C A R D ■ D E A C O N ■ A S S
L I E U ■ O R I O L E ■ T A O
E R N O ■ T I M B E R W O L F
A L E ■ D E C A ■ D O N U T
R I G ■ E L A T E S ■ M A T E
E N A M E L S ■ T U M B L E R
R E D O ■ ■ ■ S T E T ■ ■
■ S E C R E T S E R V I C E
■ ■ F L O W ■ ■ ■ S O M A
P A S S K E Y ■ L O S T D O G
I D O L ■ E S T A T E ■ E T E
M O L A R ■ A N T E ■ N I L
P R O V I D E N C E ■ R A C E
L E N ■ B I G G E R ■ A M O S
E D S ■ S P O O R S ■ Y E N S
```

80–81

```
A C T T W O ■ A B U ■ E A R S
R E H E A R ■ I O L A N T H E
I N E S S E ■ D O N T S T O P
E T E ■ T O M ■ T A E ■ I D A
T R A D E ■ I C E S ■ B R E L
T I R E ■ Y A L E ■ P R E S S
A S T R ■ A M I ■ D U O ■ ■
■ T H I N K I N G A B O U T
■ ■ D O S ■ T O V ■ K L E E
H O N E D ■ D O L E ■ E T N A
O X E S ■ S A N D ■ A D I O S
O F T ■ S A Y ■ A B M ■ M R I
T O M O R R O W ■ O N B A S E
I R A N I A N S ■ R I A T A S
E D N A ■ H E W ■ G O N E X T
```

12–13

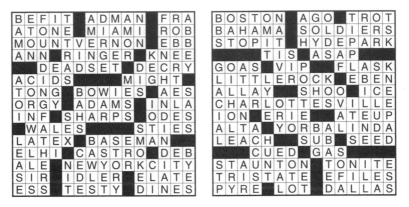

```
B E F I T   A D M A N   F R A
A T O N E   M I A M I   R O B
M O U N T V E R N O N   E B B
A N N   R I N G E R   K N E E
    D E A D S E T   D E C R Y
A C I D S       M I G H T
T O N G   B O W I E S   A E S
O R G Y   A D A M S   I N L A
I N F   S H A R P S   O D E S
  W A L E S       S T I E S
L A T E X   B A S E M A N
E L H I   C A S T R O   D E B
A L E   N E W Y O R K C I T Y
S I R   I D L E R   E L A T E
E S S   T E S T Y   D I N E S
```

22–23

```
B O S T O N   A G O   T R O T
B A H A M A   S O L D I E R S
S T O P I T   H Y D E P A R K
      T I S   A S A P
G O A S   V I P   F L A S K
L I T T L E R O C K   E B E N
A L L A Y   S H O O   I C E
C H A R L O T T E S V I L L E
I O N   E R I E   A T E U P
A L T A   Y O R B A L I N D A
L E A C H   S U B   S E E D
    C U E D   G A S
S T A U N T O N   T O N I T E
T R I S T A T E   E F I L E S
P Y R E   L O T   D A L L A S
```

32–33

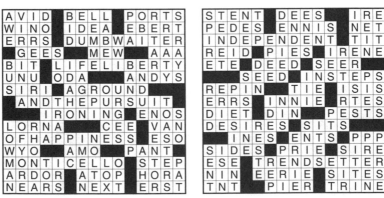

```
A V I D   B E L L   P O R T S
W I N O   I D E A   E B E R T
E R R S   D U M B W A I T E R
  G E E S   M E W   A A A
B I T   L I F E L I B E R T Y
U N U   O D A   A N D Y S
S I R I   A G R O U N D
  A N D T H E P U R S U I T
  I R O N I N G   E N O S
L O R N A   C E E   V A N
O F H A P P I N E S S   E S O
W Y O   A M O   P A N T
M O N T I C E L L O   S T E P
A R D O R   A T O P   H O R A
N E A R S   N E X T   E R S T
```

42–43

```
S T E N T   D E E S   I R E
P E D E S   E N N I S   N E T
I N D E P E N D E N T   T I T
R E I D   P I E S   I R E N E
E T E   D E E D   S E E R
    S E E D   I N S T E P S
R E P I N   T I E   I S I S
E R R S   I N N I E   R T E S
D I E T   D I N   P E S T S
D E S I R E S   S I T S
  I N E S   E N T S   P P P
S I D E S   P R I E   S I R E
E S E   T R E N D S E T T E R
N I N   E E R I E   S I T E S
T N T   P I E R   T R I N E
```

52–53

```
A L F A   S I A M   S L A T E
M O O G   I N L A   T E N E T
B A R R   T H I R T E E N T H
I N T E N S E   Y A N K E E S
      S E A   A S T R O
S M U   I N T W O   S T R O M
T E M P L E   E D U   R E P O
A N T I   S L E D S   O P E N
F L E E   T O P   E N D U R E
F O R D S   G E E S E   B A Y
        P E C A N   T I L
A L A B A M A   T E S T I N G
G E T T Y S B U R G   I C O N
E S T E E   I K E A   N A N A
S T A N D   N E E D   A N E W
```

62–63

```
D O P E D   O H I O   R A T
O N A I R   B R A V A   E R R
H E N R Y C A R T E R   E L I
    D E M O N I C   I D E A
D D E   O W E N H A R D I N G
R E M A P S   T O A T E E
A S I S   C A R O B
M I C H A E L V A N B U R E N
        S L E E P   R I P A
A T T A C H   B O N N E T
C Y N T H I A F O R D   G E E
A L O E   G I B E D A T
D E T   A N N F I L L M O R E
I R E   B R E T T   O I N K S
A S S   E A S Y   T R E O S
```

72–73

```
O B I   P A N I C   E L G I N
C E O   A T A L L   L A R G E
H E W A S T H E O N L Y O N E
S T A R T   S U E   W I S
      M O C S   T O T A L T O
B A B Y R U T H   O L S E N
E D U   R E I S S U E
T O S E R V E T W O T E R M S
    C O E R C E R   R I O
C A R R Y   H A R R I S O N
A R O U S E S   R Y E S
P G S   O L E   D I R G E
O U T O F S U C C E S S I O N
N E E D A   S H A D E   D I D
E R R E D   H O N D A   E N S
```

82–83

```
M E T E   C H A S M   F A K E
O L A V   H A D T O   I C E D
R O S E G A R D E N   G E R T
O P T   A O K   R O M A N O V
S E E R S   R E S O R T S
E S S E   E W E   S O R E N
      V A R I E T A L   I N U
N E W S C O N F E R E N C E S
A Y E   C O D E N A M E
T E N S E   R O B   T A R P
    S T E N O G S   A S T O R
R O S E T T A   A P R   O S O
E R O S   H U R R I C A N E S
D E F T   E Z I N E   D A T E
A S T O   R Y D E R   S L O T
```

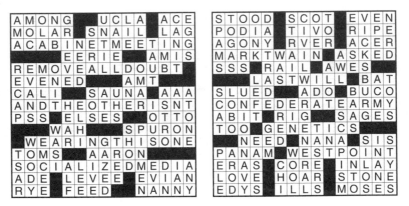

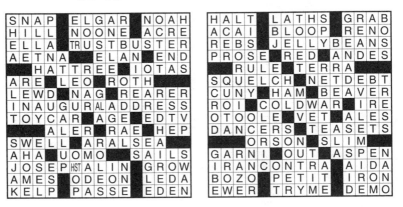

54–55

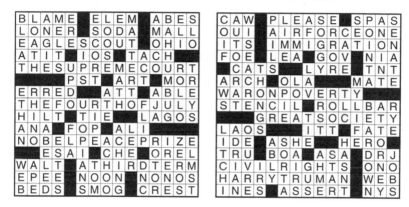

```
B L A M E   E L E M   A B E S
L O N E R   S O D A   M A L L
E A G L E S C O U T   O H I O
A T I T   I O S   T A C H
T H E S U P R E M E C O U R T
      P S T   A R T   M O R
E R R E D   A T T   A B L E
T H E F O U R T H O F J U L Y
H I L T   T I E   L A G O S
A N A   F O P   A L I
N O B E L P E A C E P R I Z E
    E S A I   C H E   O R E L
W A L T   A T H I R D T E R M
E P E E   N O O N   N O N O S
B E D S   S M O G   C R E S T
```

64–65

```
C A W   P L E A S E   S P A S
O U I   A I R F O R C E O N E
I T S   I M M I G R A T I O N
F O E   L E A   G O V   N I A
  C A T S   L Y R E   T N T
A R C H   O L A   M A T E
W A R O N P O V E R T Y
S T E N C I L   R O L L B A R
    G R E A T S O C I E T Y
L A O S   I T T   F A T E
I D E   A S H E   H E R O
T R U   B O A   A S A   D R J
C I V I L R I G H T S   O N O
H A R R Y T R U M A N   W E B
I N E S   A S S E R T   N Y S
```

74–75

```
J A G S   G A M E S   O R G S
A L O E   O B A M A   P A R A
P I L E   N O T I L L E G A L
A N D   S E V E R   I R E N E
N E W T A X E S   F E A S T S
    A B U T   T A D
S A T O N   J A I L   A R A L
T H E N A T I O N A L D E B T
Y A R D   I N K Y   E A S E D
    S E X   L A M P
A R T H U R   O V E R S E A S
T E H E E   P R E S S   C I A
T H E I R N A M E S   A T O B
I O U S   A G A P E   C E L L
C E N T   T E N S E   E D I E
```

84–85

```
A N T S   M A A M S   G A R B
G O R E   A L F I E   U V E A
A R I A   S O R E R   N O U N
P U B L I C F I N A N C I N G
E N E   R O T C   C O D E S
    H O T   A A R O N
B I D E N   I N R E   T I M E
A R E A   O B A M A   R O A M
T E L L   D E M S   C O S T S
    T A S T E   M I L
S T A H L   R I O T   S H E
C H I C A G O I L L I N O I S
R O M A   A R C E D   A N N S
U S E R   I N A N E   P I T A
B E D E   T O N E D   E A S Y
```

ABOUT THE AUTHOR

Jake Berkowitz

DAVID J. KAHN's crossword puzzles appear in *The New York Times* and many other publications. In 1997, President Bill Clinton, a big crossword fan, talked about one of Kahn's Sunday *Times* puzzles, "Technophobe's Delight," during a White House news conference on technology and the Internet.

Kahn has also written puzzles for the Clinton Presidential Library, the Walt Disney Company, the New York Yankees, and the World Science Festival. In 2005, he wrote a puzzle for the American Crossword Puzzle Tournament that was featured in the 2006 documentary *Wordplay*. His books include *Sit & Solve Baseball Crosswords* and *The Metropolitan Opera: Crosswords for Opera Lovers*.